D0407489

WITHDRAWN

LOYALTIES

HARCOURT BRACE JOVANOVICH, *Publishers*

San Diego   New York   London

DANIEL PATRICK MOYNIHAN

Loyalties

Requests for permission to make copies of any
part of the work should be mailed to:
Permissions, Harcourt Brace Jovanovich, Publishers,
Orlando, Florida 32887.

Library of Congress Cataloging in Publication Data
Moynihan, Daniel P. (Daniel Patrick), 1927–
Loyalties.
1. International law.   2. United States—Foreign
relations—1945–   .   3. United Nations—Israel.
4. Developing areas—Foreign relations.   5. United States
—Military policy   6. Arms race.   I. Title.
JX3096.M64   1984   327.73   83-22666
ISBN 0-15-154748-3

Designed by Joy Chu
Printed in the United States of America
First edition
A B C D E

FOR JAMES Q. WILSON

ACKNOWLEDGMENTS

I am uncommonly indebted to my publisher, William Jovanovich, who found a structure of thought, or so he hopes, in what was mostly a late summer and early autumn's musing. Vicki Bear bore with me on the manuscript. My son Timothy Patrick Moynihan, as copy editor, was a kindly disciplinarian.

CONTENTS

ONE

Launch on Warning

On July 26, 1983, two weeks of debate came to a close in the Senate on the question of authorizing funds for the procurement and deployment of MX missiles in existing Minuteman silos in Wyoming and Nebraska. Although the "X" denotes experimental, this most formidable weapon was already fully developed and ready to be produced. A land-based intercontinental ballistic missile was begun as a conventional weapon in the sense that it was intended to continue the "triad" mode of American nuclear arms: land-based missiles, long-range bombers, and nuclear submarines. The need for the new missile arose when the Soviet Union developed its own intercontinental ballistic missile force to a level where in a "first strike" it could probably destroy our land-based missiles. This was the conceptual focus of the argument, along with the fact that the Soviets had begun to "harden" their own missile fields, such that the prospect of an American second strike was losing its deterrent effect. The Omnibus Defense Authorization Act authorized $2.536 billion for the procurement of twenty-seven MX missiles—of which twenty-one were for actual operational deployment, six for spares and tests. These were to be the first of 100 such missiles to be procured and deployed.

Although the President had indicated 100 would be the limit, it was known that Air Force planners were thinking of going well beyond this number. On July 10, Senator Gary Hart of Colorado had announced he would engage in "extended debate" on the floor of the Senate to seek to delete this item. It had not been a filibuster in the traditional sense of trying to prevent a vote from taking place. Rather, it was, for the half dozen of us taking part, an effort to make the Senate realize that it was about to commit the most profound mistake in the history of America's nuclear weapons. We were, with this vote, moving from a strategy of deterrence to a condition of "launch on warning."

As a military strategy, deterrence has the inestimable advantage of being simple. Its principles are few, and when in place they are seen to be in place. This is to say that the world, and especially the Soviets, can observe that we are keeping to our avowed strategy. If we are not, then that, too, is instantly on display. It is, in this sense, the strategy of an honest power, one that wishes to be trusted, and denies itself the ability to deceive.

No. . . . On a moment's reflection that statement goes too far. The ability to deceive is inherent in the technology of intercontinental nuclear weapons. A decision to strike first and destroy an adversary can be made, and there is no way the adversary can know about it, except through the unlikely presence of an enemy agent in the War Room. Let me define it once more. The essential characteristic of deterrence as a strategic doctrine is that it does not put a nation under a *compulsion* to deceive.

In point of fact, in the 1950s, when the United States had a great nuclear superiority over the Soviets, some studies did advocate a first-strike strategy. President Dwight D. Eisenhower rejected this and gradually the doctrine of deterrence evolved. This doctrine accepted the fact that the Soviets would have a nuclear capacity, and a large one, but undertook to ensure that the United States would also have nuclear forces, these deployed in such a manner that a surprise attack could only destroy *a portion of them*—after which an American second strike would prove utterly devastating to the enemy. In that situation, no rational head of state or military commander would commence a nuclear exchange.

Under Eisenhower, the Minutemen were authorized and soon deployed in fixed silos on the high Western plains. It was thought that these, along with the B-52 bomber and the Polaris submarine, would about do it. A revealing truth is that American nuclear weapons today are just about the same as those ordered up by Eisenhower. Of course, there have been improvements. Of the 1,000 deployed Minuteman missiles, 450 still have single warheads, but 550 have been fitted with multiple reentry vehicles (MIRVs) and they carry three warheads. But the present missiles are of the same family as the originals. Similarly, the B-52 has been improved, but remains the same plane; many of the B-52s are older than the pilots who fly them. Only at sea have we gone on to an entirely new submarine, the Trident, and its wholly new missile, the D-5, which will be operational by the end of this decade.

Now, it had been widely thought that what the Soviets wanted with respect to American nuclear power was some rough equivalence to the U.S. There is an "asymmetry" in our forces, the Soviets being a land power, the U.S. a sea power. Exact equivalence is an inexact idea. But rough equivalence—yes, we can speak of it. Toward the end of the 1960s the Soviets were clearly on the way to such parity.

The trouble is that they did not stop with parity. Their number of nuclear warheads on intercontinental forces went from the low hundreds in 1965 on a straight trajectory to almost 8,000 in 1982. In response, American warheads, which had been declining in numbers in the late 1960s, shot up to the 9,000 level by 1982. But in the meantime the Soviets had *passed* the United States in two measures of strength.

About 1972, their steadily mounting megatonnage (the cumulative explosive power of their warheads) passed ours, which had been declining, and the Soviets kept going. At about that time, also, their total number of strategic nuclear delivery vehicles, mostly missiles, passed that of the United States. Each missile was newer, bigger, better. I recall in 1969 and 1970 a thoroughly informed Melvin R. Laird, as Secretary of Defense, informing the Nixon Cabinet that the Soviets didn't seem to want to stop testing new missiles. What is more, each appeared to be bigger and more powerful or more versatile than the last. After a period of testing, they would go straight into production and deployment.

It began to dawn on everyone that the Minuteman silos and those of the old Titans were becoming vulnerable to a first strike. If "taken out" in a surprise attack, we would have no land-based missiles to launch the deterrent second strike. There seemed no choice: A new missile would have to be developed if deterrence was to be maintained.

And so the search began for a basing mode compatible with deterrence doctrine, and so also the fact began to emerge that the new weapon was too big for this to be possible.

The MX is a SALT missile, which is to say, a product of the particular constraints of that particular arms control agreement. Granted our limited experience with such agreements, they would appear to have this effect. The naval treaties of the 1920s produced the pocket battleship, which is to say, the strike power of a battleship crammed into the hull of a cruiser. In just this way the SALT I agreement, by limiting the number and size of launch vehicles, rather than, say, the number of warheads, or their explosive power, rewarded the party that could pack the most destructive power into a single missile of a given size. Specifically, it rewarded the Soviet Union's decision to build the huge SS-18. Combined with improvements in accuracy, this ICBM became the basis on which claims were made that our static-based Minuteman missiles were vulnerable to a first strike. To offset this imbalance in strategic capabilities and yet remain within the constraints of the SALT process, the MX was conceived. The result, however, was a missile too large to conceal, and too "valuable" not to be targeted, thus weakening the structure of deterrence even as it sought to advance it. (These are in fact weapons *systems* with an internal, essentially mathematical coherence. As we began to depart from the "configuration" of deterrence doctrine with respect to missile deployment, we also began to retreat from earlier doctrine that forbade anti-missile defense. We had renounced such defenses in the ABM treaty. As will be touched upon, we now begin to think of them anew.)

Over the course of a decade, some thirty-four possible basing modes for the MX were considered by the Department of Defense. In an official listing, they were:

1. Launch Under Attack (LUA).
2. Orbital Based.
3. Shallow Underwater Missile (SUM).
4. Hydra.
5. Off-Shore Recoverable Capsule, Anchored (ORCA).
6. Ship—Inland.
7. Ship—Ocean.
8. Sea Sitter.
9. Wide Body Jet (WBJ).
10. Short Takeoff and Landing (STOL).

11. Vertical Takeoff and Landing (VTOL).
12. Dirigible.
13. Midgetman.
14. Hard Rock Silo.
15. Hard Tunnel.
16. South Side Basing.
17. Sandy Silo.
18. Commercial Rail.
19. Dedicated Rail.
20. Off-Road Mobile.
21. Ground Effect Machine (GEM).
22. Road Mobile (Minuteman).
23. Road Mobile (New Missile).
24. Covered Trench.
25. Hybrid Trench.
26. Dash to Shelter.
27. Mobile Front End.
28. POOL.
29. Minuteman/MPS.
30. MX/MPS.
31. Continuous Airborne Aircraft.
32. Deep Underground Basing.
33. Ballistic Missile Defense (BMD).
34. Dense Pack.

Somewhere in the process of considering all these schemes a leakage of reality occurred. Carter's military advisers, and the President himself, had seriously believed it would be possible to build option Number 30, multiple protective shelters, or the "racetrack," as it came to be known. They had no notion of using the new missile as a "bargaining chip" in some forthcoming arms negotiation. It was meant to be a permanent fixture of the triad, deployed on rails, moving underground over vast reaches of the Far West. Even the Air Force (whose missile it was) had identified thirty-eight federal laws that would have to be complied with to build the project— and they missed the Wild, Free-Roaming Horse and Burro Act of 1971. But there had to be an MX if there was to be a SALT II treaty. I supported the treaty, but, even so, in 1979 asked whether "in a nation where nuclear power plants can no longer be built, does anyone seriously suppose that the government can dig up Utah and Nevada to put in place our largest missiles without arousing passionate opposition?"

They did. There *was* a leakage of reality. Right to the end, the Carter people thought they had solved the problem. As it happened, the best friend in the Congress of the next President was the former Governor of Nevada. The 1980 election put an unceremonious end to the "racetrack."

Next? President Reagan appointed a commission headed by the Nobel Prize physicist Charles H. Townes, which came up with basing option Number 34, dense pack. As described by the report of the Armed Services Committee that accompanied the Omnibus Defense Authorization Act, this concept relied on the "phenomenon known as 'fratricide'—whereby attacking warheads would, because of the proximity of their targets to one another and the size of the weapons needed to destroy those targets, destroy or degrade each other's effectiveness." This was proposed to Congress on November 22, 1982, to the accompaniment of whatever passes for hilarity in the discussion of nuclear strategy. "Duncepack" was doomed from the outset, and for a singularly important reason.

At most, one person in the Senate—I cannot speak for the House—could claim a minimal grasp of the physics involved and could guess what "fratricide" involved, what "cratering" effects might be expected, and so on. That person was Senator Harrison H. Schmitt of New Mexico, a former astronaut and geologist. Schmitt was the only scientist in the Senate then—the only one in our history. But he had been defeated for re-election. Dense pack was rejected because it didn't seem to make sense and had been given a funny name. Had Thomas Jefferson been Vice President and presiding, the debate would at least have been more open to the possibilities of science. The Senate had, and still has, no capacity for making complex scientific judgments; and it shows little patience with the seemingly unending statistical quarreling that is so natural to the life of science.

On December 16, 1982, a motion by the late Senator Henry M. Jackson of Washington was adopted providing funds for procurement of MX missiles but prohibiting any expenditure until such time as an alternative basing mode had been explicitly approved by both houses of Congress. Jackson's amendment was adopted 56 to 42 and was left substantially intact by the conference committee. On January 3, 1983, the President appointed a Commission on Strategic Forces, headed by a distinguished military officer and former National Security Advisor to President Ford, Air Force Lieutenant General Brent Scowcroft. In the meantime, he had named the missile "Peacekeeper." (It was reported that the name was inspired by a six-gun on display in the office of his then National Security Advisor. The decision moved one journalist to describe the setting: "on a bookshelf in the modest White House basement office of William P. Clark . . . there rests a United States marshal's badge and a Colt .45, known in the old West as 'the Peacemaker.' Today, the gun, once used by Mr. Clark's grandfather against cattle rustlers in California, serves as a symbol of peace through strength in American foreign policy.")

A significant number of the eleven members of the

Scowcroft Commission did not share President Reagan's conviction that the United States faced a "window of vulnerability," through which our land-based missiles could be hit by a Soviet first strike, such that our deterrent was no longer effective, and would not be until survivable new land-based missiles were in place.

The Commission found, to the contrary, that if the Soviets were simultaneously to attack the strategic bomber forces with low-trajectory submarine-launched missiles *and* the missiles fields with ICBMs, the bombers would be hit first, thereby alerting the missiles in time for them to get off. If the attack were timed for simultaneous arrival, the ICBM warning system would give the bombers time to get off. These intervals involved "over a quarter of an hour." The Commission went on to make a major strategic proposal. In effect, it proposed that we abandon the huge, MIRVed land-based missiles set in silos, which made up the second weapons system of the nuclear age, following the bomber. Technology had either leapt upon them or crept up on them; in any event, they were irreducibly vulnerable and therefore useless as a deterrent—in short, not a reliable second strike. The Commission proposed we move instead to a force of light, single-warhead, probably mobile weapons—the Midgetman, as it came to be called. (Note, this was the thirteenth of the thirty-four basing options considered since 1972.)

But stop. They did not stop there. Between April 1983 and the time a force of Midgetman missiles was in place, there would indeed be the *political* problem of learning to live with a new and real Soviet threat. And so to solve the *political* problem, and produce a unanimous report, the panel proposed to deploy the MX in existing Minuteman silos, which could only have the effect of vastly exacerbating that very problem.

The reasoning with respect to Midgetman was flaw-less.

The Commission submitted its report in April 1983. However singular the subject—life on the planet—the outcome was lamentably familiar as a *type* of government report. Experts of impeccable credentials are appointed to solve a political problem disguised as a technical one. Their technical advice was superb, their political solution calamitous. In effect, the panel agreed that American strategic forces did indeed face a period of danger in the 1980s as our old weapons became ever more vulnerable to Soviet new weapons. Their answer was to develop and deploy a small, mobile, single-warhead "Midgetman" missile, which could be available by the end of the decade. That comported with every strategic and technical stricture. The experts had given their expert opinion and it was just that.

Such a missile "inherently denies an attacker the opportunity to destroy more than one warhead with one attacking warhead." This is the *essence* of the idea of deterrence: Make attack difficult and response inevitable. The Commission judged that such a missile, "hardened against nuclear effects," was well within the range of current technology. It proposed that we proceed to full-scale development by 1987 and to deployment in the early 1990s.

To say again, this was superb. But then, of a sudden, the tone of the report changed. Having learned there was no "window of vulnerability" that urgently needed to be closed by the ninety-five ton, ten-warhead MX, and that a small, mobile, fifteen-ton one-warhead substitute would be much better, we were told that that MX should nonetheless be built and, further, placed in the very Minuteman silos which, having become vulnerable a decade earlier, had set the Air Force off in search for a successor. In sum: there was no window of vulnerability, but proceed nonetheless to deploy the MXs to close it. And put them in the place most vulnerable to attack.

And why? Because we had to be careful of the "Soviets' perception of our national will and cohesion." It was suggested that we got an Anti-Ballistic Missile Treaty out of them in 1972 because we had maintained an "ongoing ABM program." The MX program would be an equivalent inducement for another arms treaty. What is more, we had already spent over $5 billion on the damn thing.

One day, a history will no doubt be written of the Scowcroft Commission. I write of its aftermath. The Congress was instantly divided. It was 1983. The nuclear freeze movement had begun, a mass movement dealing with a subject that theretofore had been kept within the closest circles of the universities and the government. In the nice phrase of Representative Albert Gore, Jr., "Congress . . . [had] changed. Because of the freeze, there [was] now some of the same sense of nuance and detail in nuclear matters that formerly was reserved for tax laws and highway construction bills."

More important, because more specific, the American Catholic Bishops had issued their Pastoral Letter on War and Peace, *The Challenge of Peace: God's Promise and Our Response.* Here, the reader is entitled to know, I write as a Roman Catholic. What precisely or, rather, what generally do I mean by that? I do not consider myself bound by the pastoral letter; and as a Catholic I am not. I am bound to pay attention, but I feel equally bound to pay attention to what sometime colleagues such as Paul Doty, Samuel P. Huntington, Albert Carnesale, and Jack Ruina think. I try to follow what Albert

Wohlstetter thinks. I pay attention to what other Senators think. But the Bishops' letter addressed itself to the moral issues of nuclear weapons. No statement of such weight had done this before. It spoke from a long tradition, "reaching from the Sermon on the Mount," and from a long involvement with the politics of succeeding ages.

They spoke as bishops, but also as *American* bishops. They would not "pretend that as a nation we have lived up to all our own ideals." To do that would be "patently dishonest." To pretend that all the evils in the present world can be traced to dictatorships, however, "would be both dishonest and absurd." But, having said this, they went on to insist that it was "imperative" to confront the larger reality: "The facts simply do not support the invidious comparisons made at times even in our own society between our way of life, in which most basic human rights are at least recognized even if they are not always adequately supported, and those totalitarian and tyrannical regimes in which such rights are either denied or systematically suppressed."

The Bishops had not been comfortable with the concept of deterrence. In 1979, testifying on behalf of the ratification of the SALT II treaty, John Cardinal Krol of Philadelphia granted that the U.S. strategic doctrine of deterrence may in fact have prevented nuclear warfare, but added that "the risk of failure and the physical harm and moral evil resulting from possible nuclear war remained." This, he said, "explains the Catholic dissatisfaction with nuclear deterrence and the urgency of the Catholic demand that the nuclear arms race be reversed." In just this vein, in their 1983 pastoral letter, the Bishops concluded that the teaching of the Church, and "applying it through our own prudential judgement, lead us to a strictly conditioned moral acceptance of nuclear deterrence."

And they would be right. The bombers are airborne twenty-four hours a day, the year round; the missile crews are on duty, the submarines at sea. Everywhere, officers wait for the word, devising ever more locked-in procedures to make sure it *is* the word. Everywhere, the lights flicker, the green-yellow scopes fill with bouncing lines, waving lines, sweeping lines. The trigger is at hand. It is just that deterrence, to paraphrase Churchill, is the worst strategy save any other.

My own problems with the MX were deep-seated. From the first, the MX had been developed as a "counter-force" weapon, which is to say a missile that could strike at and "take out" the missiles of the Soviet Union. This would not have threatened "crisis stability"—the utterly essential consideration—if the Soviets had chosen actually to imitate the Americans in nuclear matters—the proposition behind the celebrated image of "two apes on a treadmill." But they had not deployed their forces in a deterrent mode, as we had done. The size and number of their missiles could only imply a first-strike mode. This is to say, they are right out there in plain view, essentially undefended. They are highly, if not wholly, vulnerable to a first strike from the United States, but so long as the United States did not have a weapon capable of such a mission, the Soviets could, if they chose, keep calm. And they did. They kept on building, but not in a fit of panic.

At about the time Cardinal Krol testified in 1979, I was writing a long article for *The New Yorker* addressing my own, and similar, misgivings. It had seemed to me that by linking the MX to the Salt II treaty the Carter administration had begun to compromise our previous understanding of deterrence as basic nuclear strategy. The MX missile, I wrote, "is incompatible with the doctrine. . . . It is, as its advocates in the Administration like to say, a 'hard-target-kill counterforce weapon.'" That is what we had told ourselves a deterrent force does *not* have. Thus, we would be "building the missile that undermines the doctrine in order to sustain the doctrine. A paradox? Yes." And more: the makings of ruin.

Deterrence solved the seemingly insoluble problem of preventing the use of nuclear weapons. But it had assumed the Soviets would see the logic of our solution—and do as we did. As it turned out, the problem was not that the Soviets imitated us, but that they did not. And it mattered little what we professed, for all that would matter to them was that we were now seemingly intent on deploying a missile capable, in sufficient numbers, of wiping out their land-based forces, and accordingly putting both systems on a hair trigger.

By mid-1979, it was clear the Salt II treaty was not going to pass the Senate. A group of us who met to discuss tactics for getting it through never counted more than forty votes in the Senate in favor of the treaty, and I, for one, could not count twenty. With no treaty, the administration would not press the MX, which was to have been a kind of reward in exchange for the treaty. Besides, I knew about the Wild, Free-Roaming Horse and Burro Act of 1971. Indeed, well before the fate of the treaty was settled, I had told then Majority Leader Robert Byrd that the MX would never be built, meaning that the racetrack would never be built. So much for *my* foresight.

Four years passed. Of a sudden the MX was not only going to be built, but also going to be deployed in the most unstable mode that could be devised. *What had happened?* Nothing much. A new President. A new Chairman of the Senate Armed Services Committee. (No change in the House.) A Commission. Everyday life in the capital. There was no new information. Yet here we were seemingly intent on making the most profound change in nuclear strategy in our history.

But now to the event of July 26, 1983. The outcome of the "gentle filibuster" was never in doubt. The votes, as we say, were there; if Senator John Tower, Chairman the Armed Services Committee, at times seemed impatient, it was because he knew this. A test vote on the MX had been taken in the Senate on May 26, and had succeeded, 59 to 39. On July 20, by a vote of 220 to 207 the House of Representatives had already approved an authorization bill embodying the Scowcroft recommendations. President Reagan had promised House Democrats that with MX funding behind him, he would feel free to take new initiatives in the frozen strategic arms control talks in Geneva.

Even so, such an enormity had to be addressed, even if it took two weeks, including the vast inconvenience of a Saturday session in July. The point was that we were submitting to a change in a strategy of more than twenty years' standing. For twenty years we had said that we would absorb a full nuclear strike before firing back. This was a strategy that had been our claim to a margin of moral superiority over the Soviet Union despite the accumulation by both nations of weapons and weapons systems of incredible—no, credible—destructiveness.

The alternative strategic doctrine—other than a deliberate first-strike policy—is "launch on warning." "Launch under attack" is a slightly different way of saying the same thing. Note that in the listing of the various deployment modes that had been considered for the MX, launch under attack had been first. It was promptly rejected, or so we may assume. But even at the outset, it was clear how difficult it would be to find a survivable deployment mode for such huge missiles. Technology was making them too easy to find and to destroy.

Now, the Soviets did have 308 SS-18s and 300 SS-19s, weapons roughly comparable to the MX, meaning capable of destroying it in the open. This was indisputable at an analytic level. (No one knows just how well any of these weapons would work in an actual nuclear exchange. There has never been one.) This being so, the Reagan administration, shifting from the Carter position, contended that the MX was needed as a bargaining chip. It was asserted, in effect, that by acting in a wildly dangerous and threatening manner, we would bring the Soviets to their senses on arms control. The formal report of the Armed Services Committee, dated July 5, stated that deploying the MX in Minuteman silos was "the only significant near-term action which will induce the Soviets to negotiate." This verges on an official lie. The staff person who wrote it did not think he was lying; and the persons he heard it from did not think they were lying. But we know nothing of our age if we do not know that governments routinely declare they need more arms in order to ensure peace. *Sometimes this is true.* More often it is a lie. It is part of the grammar of official lying, and has no place in a report of a committee of the United States Senate. It is not as if anybody in Washington knew what will or will not induce the Soviet leaders to behave one way or another way.

What we do know is that these missiles, the most powerful and accurate we had ever developed, would be deployed in a mode so vulnerable as practically to invite a preemptive Soviet strike. This is central to the issue of "crisis stability," a concern that began at least with the Cuban missile crisis of 1962, and the subsequent vast expansion of Soviet forces. The principal goal of crisis stability is to ensure, as much as possible, that in a crisis that might lead to war each party is reasonably confident that it will not be destroyed by a preemptive strike by the other party. Communication is essential, or would reasonably seem to be. The "hot line" between Washington and Moscow was installed after the 1962 missile crisis.

For some time, a breakfast group of Senators had been discussing enlarging on this now "ancient" initiative. New kinds of crises could be envisioned. In a "for-instance" scenario, suppose an Iraqi pilot in an F-15 fighter-bomber captured from the Israelis or borrowed from the Saudis, prompted by some official or personal motive to wreak havoc, drops a nuclear device on Sevastopol. The outward evidence is overwhelming: The United States has commenced pre-emptive nuclear war. How are the Soviets to be persuaded this is not so? How, in the reverse circumstances, is the United States to be persuaded? Good questions. Senators Sam Nunn of Georgia and the late Henry M. Jackson proposed that a kind of joint military staff group be set up somewhere in the world to monitor events around the clock, such that if some bizarre accident or intrigue occurred it might be jointly confirmed, such that both parties would act from the same information.

The one source of crisis instability, however, which no amount of communication can overcome is the possession by *both* parties of "hard-target, kill-capable" missiles that are targeted toward opposing missiles *but vulnerable themselves to destruction by a first strike*. The phrase is "Use 'em, or lose 'em." That is precisely the situation that will come into being the moment the MX is deployed in the Minuteman silos, each one of which has, for some years now, been targeted by two Soviet warheads. (Such warheads are said to be "dedicated.") In a crisis, the Soviets will know that we know they can destroy our land-based missile force in a first strike—and that we will be thinking about using them before losing them.

It is known that the Soviets practice this situation as a war game. The "Canadian Geese Problem" is the most difficult one to solve. That is to say: are you certain the radar is showing you a flight of missiles, or could it be a flight of arctic birds? Or could the radar be on the blink, or the computer malfunctioning? The obvious way to deal with this is the equivalent of layered defense. First one line of radars, then another. When enough check out with identical information, a decision must be made in the time remaining.

In my final exchange in the debate with Senator Tower, I asked if he would care to estimate how much time that would be. Two days? Obviously not. Two hours? Of course not. Twenty minutes? He responded that we would have to close the Senate chamber to speak further of such sensitive matters, but yes, of course, it was a matter of minutes. Allow me to reveal what everyone knows. With a layered radar-screen system, an attack having been confirmed, there would be eight to twelve minutes to decide whether to counterattack. That is not enough time, and argues, in a crisis, for taking no chances and striking first. If, that is, the adversary has vulnerable weapons such as the MX in the Minuteman silos.

Senator Tower spoke to the facts of the matter; others went further. At about this time, in the highest circles of the Senate, it was becoming fashionable to assert that should ever the Soviets start a war we will want our silos to be empty when their missiles arrive. Nuclear strategists use the term "breakout" to describe a sudden technological advance in a weapons system or a change in a balance of forces that disturbs the equilibrium of power.

Something such had happened with respect to the formulation of nuclear strategy itself. This had been the domain of intellectuals; in the main, academics; economists mostly. A cloistered world. Perhaps the three most influential theorists in the development of deterrence doctrine still active are Albert J. Wohlstetter, Henry S. Rowen, and Fred S. Hoffman. None will be found in *Who's Who in America*. But with the breakout, strategies began to be devised at rallies, and also in cloakrooms. In the latter, deterrence seemed far too passive, too brainy a posture. "Use 'em or lose 'em" was the fact of the matter and that meant launch on warning.

And so the Senate proceeded to vote. First on the amendment of Senator Hart, which would delete all funds for the procurement and deployment of the MX; it was lost, 58 to 41. Second, and finally, I offered an amendment to delete only funds for deployment. We reasoned this would be a test of just how much faith the majority had in the "bargaining-chip" theory. (By majority, I mean those supporting the Committee bill. This was close to, but not quite, a party division. Seven Republicans voted for both Hart's amendment and mine.) If the majority really did believe in the bargaining chip, why not build the missiles, put them in a warehouse, photograph them, give the photographs to the Soviet negotiators in Geneva with the statement that if no arms reduction agreement is reached, the missiles will forthwith be lowered into the Minuteman silos, or wherever? This seemingly logical proposition earned us one additional vote, that of Senator Lawton Chiles of Florida. My amendment lost, 57 to 42. On final passage of the bill, the vote was 83 to 15.

For the first time since coming to the Senate, I voted against a defense bill. The MX provision seemed to me intolerable. Fourteen others agreed. But the great majority of Senators was prepared to live with the decision. If nothing changes, the first ten MXs will be in their silos at Warren Air Force Base in Wyoming in time for Christmas 1986.

The irony is that the Senate knew that even as we were putting more of our forces in a fixed, ICBM mode, the Soviets were beginning to diversify their arsenal, recognizing the vulnerability of such fixed sites, possibly concerned with stability in a crisis, but in any event already developing a mobile land-based missile, much as the Scowcroft Commission recommended that we do.

Specifically, they had begun testing a small, single-warhead, presumedly mobile missile, which we had named the PL-5 (after the Soviet test range at Plesetsk). It is just possible that they, too, realize that the age of the giant ICBM may be passing. It is just possible they are beginning to think about deterrence in the American mode, as exemplified in the Midgetman proposal put forth by the Scowcroft Commission. In the debate, I referred repeatedly to the testing of the PL-5 and this possibility.

If further irony is needed, a case can be made that Ronald Reagan was the first President to come to office with an informed sense that the structure of arms limitation agreements and talks with the Soviets was not working at all well. Salt I, agreed to in 1972, had seemingly not at all impeded the growth of weaponry. Salt II, agreed to in 1979, promised little more.

On August 1, 1979, I had accordingly proposed an amendment to the SALT II treaty. As negotiated, the final article called upon the parties to effect "significant and substantial reductions in the number of strategic offensive arms" in the *next* treaty. My amendment provided that these reductions should be agreed to by December 31, 1981, *or else SALT II would expire.* SALT II had a protocol forbidding the deployment of certain cruise missiles before that date. It was thus a logical midpoint at which to test the Soviet willingness actually to *reduce* nuclear weapons and of the United States not to introduce a new weapons system—the Cruise.

Neither the Senate nor official Washington was much impressed by my proposal. It was a curious moment. The Senate had, in effect, decided to have nothing to do with the treaty. The Carter administration, however, was altogether unaware of this. The arrogance of the previous year—the National Security Advisor would inform a dinner companion that her husband would have no choice but to vote for the agreement when it arrived—was giving way to a certain concern, but no serious alarm. The object of my amendment was to give persons in the middle a chance to vote in favor of actual reductions in strategic offensive arms, and, further, to find out if the Soviets were serious in professing to desire them.

In any event, the press took no notice. Yet a few days later, out of nowhere, you might say—actually from 10960 Wilshire Boulevard in Los Angeles—I received a telephone call from Ronald Reagan, who asked if he might see my remarks in the *Congressional Record*. I sent them along, of course, and on August 16 received a most civil letter of thanks. "We are in agreement in every major point," he wrote, adding, "I believe we should take the high ground and stand firm for arms limitation. SALT I and SALT II have resulted (or will result if SALT II is ratified) in arms increases."

That autumn the long article in *The New Yorker* titled "The SALT Process" appeared, in which I expanded on the general subject of the process producing the opposite of its intended effect—it was *not* getting us arms reduction. This is something that frequently turns up in systems analysis. I sent a copy to Governor Reagan, who again replied most graciously. "I can only tell you," he wrote, "that I am in great agreement. . . ."

Once elected, Reagan seemed to proceed on that premise. In an address on November 18, 1981, he declared that the United States was prepared to cancel its deployment of new missiles in Europe if the Soviets in turn dismantled their batteries. This, he said, "would be an historic step. With Soviet agreement, we could together substantially reduce the dread threat of nuclear war which hangs over the people of Europe. This, like the first footstep on the moon, would be a giant step for mankind." He went on to state that he had informed President Leonid Brezhnev of the Soviet Union that he hoped the soon-to-open general negotiations in Geneva would result in further reductions in levels of arms. He continued: "To symbolize this fundamental change in direction, we will call these negotiations START—Strategic Arms *Reduction* Talks."

And yet this same President two months earlier had asked for a huge increase in funds for producing nuclear warheads. The request was reduced somewhat by the appropriation committees, but for the first time the sum exceeded $1 billion. What *happened?* The 1980 Republican platform offers some explanation. Much influenced by Senator Tower, it combines a somewhat muddled statement of ethical unease over the doctrine of deterrence with a fearsome insistence on more weaponry of every sort.

In its early—and perhaps purist form—deterrence involved targeting Soviet cities, and in a sense holding their civilian populations hostage against a Soviet attack on the United States. This came to be known as Mutual Assured Destruction, with the acronym MAD. The 1980 Republican platform declared that Carter's adherence to that doctrine "limits the President during crises to a

Hobson's choice between mass mutual suicide and surrender." But, having asserted that under Carter the
United States had "moved from essential equivalence to
inferiority in strategic nuclear forces with the Soviet
Union," the platform plank promised that Republicans
would create a "credible strategy which will deter Soviet
attack" by acquiring a much greater nuclear capability,
so much that we could "survive and ultimately . . . destroy Soviet military targets." Presumedly, this meant that
deterrence would continue as doctrine, but targeting
would change and force levels would be greatly in-
creased.

The Republican platform was not so much a sinister
assertion as a frivolous one. There surely existed a moral
problem with deterrence as a form of hostage-taking. But
an undifferentiated call for more warheads was hardly
an answer. In any event, deterrence directed only at cities was no longer American policy. For some years, we
had been targeting military installations as part of a second strike. Carter had formalized this practice in a Presidential Directive. The Republicans knew this. There is
something altogether too casual about a statement that
the incumbent President's strategy limits him "during
crises to a Hobson's choice between mass mutual suicide and surrender." Hobson was an innkeeper who
rented horses, but required customers to take the one
nearest to the door. A "Hobson's choice" is no choice. If
nuclear strategy matters, it matters that it be stated ac-
curately. And as for the assertion of "inferiority," to repeat, it was not true.

Withal, administrations changed, and, at some level of
significance, nuclear affairs began to be discussed and
decided at the level of the rhetoric of the 1980 Republican platform. There is evidence that the new President
held to his early views. On June 8, 1983, Secretary of

State George P. Shultz presented to a meeting of NATO foreign ministers a report titled "Security and Arms Control: The Search for a More Stable Policy." It stressed the bipartisan nature of American arms control efforts, going back to President Truman, who, again to repeat, proposed in 1946 to eliminate nuclear weapons and turn nuclear energy over to the United Nations. Of more recent events, the report observed: "Although the SALT process brought certain benefits in the SALT I agreement, its final result as embodied in SALT II was a clear disappointment to the hopes generated in the early 1970s." Fair comment. Careful language. President Reagan had decided "it would be better to confront the problem of significantly reducing existing numbers of strategic forces rather than simply making another attempt to limit their further growth." Again: a reasoned, carefully stated position.

What, then, accounts for the MX decision? One exogenous event, as economists would say, was an article by Andrei Sakharov, in the form of an open letter to the physicist Sidney Drell, in the Summer 1983 issue of *Foreign Affairs*. Entitled "The Danger of Thermonuclear War," it nonetheless seemed to endorse deployment of the MX owing to Soviet strength in silo-based missiles: "At present the U.S.S.R. has a great advantage in this area. Perhaps talks about the limitation and reduction of these most destructive missiles could become easier if the United States were to have MX missiles, albeit only potentially (indeed, that would be best of all)." This argument was a force on the Senate floor, and my amendment—to build but not deploy—was a response.

But the outcome was not decided by argument. It was decided by routine: the routine that the Air Force had to have a new missile inasmuch as the Navy had got a new missile for its new submarine and the Army was scheduled to deploy *its* new missile, the Pershing II; the routine that the Scowcroft Commission had to reach a consensus and had used a device picked up from the Social Security Commission, which earlier that year presented its proposals as an interconnected whole that could not be disturbed; the routine that Congress never, in the end, refuses a President a new weapons system; the routine that the Armed Services Committee gets its way.

What was lacking was a sufficiently compelling sense of the principles that were at stake. What was lacking was a sense of loyalty to life. Some part of this must be ascribed to the mind-numbing effect of thinking too much about the issue. In 1782, twenty Americans died at Yorktown. Two centuries later, former Defense Secretary Harold Brown could write: "The destruction of more than 100 million people in each of the United States, the Soviet Union, and the European nations could take place during the first half-hour of nuclear war." It is human, perhaps, to want to put the issue out of mind. During 1979, I put more effort into this issue of the SALT treaty than any other. I spoke about it, wrote about it, tried to amend it. During that year I received more letters from New Yorkers on the issue of the Alaskan timber wolf than on the arms treaty.

But that is what principles are for: to inform conduct when affairs seem out of control or beyond comprehension. The vote to deploy the MX in a launch on warning mode indicated either an absence of principle or else its abandonment. There will be no return to principle unless we teach ourselves how to weigh the moral dimensions, and dilemmas, of the decisions we are required to make. As man is God's most cherished creation, so preservation of His gift of life to us must be our most urgent duty. Pope John Paul said it best, in his address at Hiroshima on February 25, 1981: "In the past, it was possible to destroy a village, a town, a region, even a country. Now it is the whole planet that has come under threat. This fact should finally compel everyone to face a basic moral consideration: *From now on, it is only through a conscious choice and through a deliberate policy that humanity can survive*" (Emphasis added).

It may fairly be said that for doctrinal intricacy and duration of debate, as well as for its enduring value, Christian theology occupies a special place in the history of ideas. From the earliest times, the debate has been characterized by men of great learning and by texts of intimidating complexity. Indeed, there could scarcely have been greater contrast than what obtained in the Middle Ages, when the higher clergy was reading and writing in ancient languages while the laity was almost entirely illiterate. Even so, through those centuries and down to the present time, theologians conceded great authority in matters of doctrine to the *sensum fidelium*, the belief of the faithful.

May I suggest that something comparable is to be encountered in the American people today in their newly aroused concern about nuclear weapons? There is in this perception of terrible danger a kind of ultimate truth, which the experts must acknowledge—and to which they ought in the end defer. Historians of the subject regularly resort to ecclesiastical analogies. In his book *Cold Dawn*, John Newhouse writes of debates that recalled "those between the Thomists and the essentially Franciscan followers of Duns Scotus." In his history *The Wizards of Armageddon*, Fred Kaplan writes of the strategic theorists of the 1950s and 1960s as "thermonuclear Jesuits."

Now the *sensum fidelium* began to be expressed. In the first four months of 1983 I heard in writing from

134,890 New Yorkers about a nuclear freeze resolution. The concern exists that a mass movement calling for nuclear arms reductions must inevitably have greater influence on the democratic party to any such negotiations than on the totalitarian party. Such a concern is not to be dismissed. Persons demanding an "immediate" end to the arms race could usefully be reminded that, in this life, good will is not always rewarded in kind. Those of a historical bent will recall that, during the Holy Year 1500, Cesare Borgia, at the head of the forces of Pope Alexander VI (who happened also to be his parent), had set out to lay siege to Camerino, in an outlying region of the Papal States. His march took him in the direction of the prosperous city of Urbino, whose Duke possessed the finest artillery in Italy at the time. Borgia asked to borrow this new weapon system, and the Duke, by all accounts a pious and scholarly man, agreed. Whereupon Borgia laid siege to Urbino instead, and forced the Duke to flee into exile.

There is a responsibility, then, to speak to this movement as well as for it. The Bishops have done this well. They remind us that nuclear war is not merely a mathematical problem of percentages and trajectories and megatonnage; that arms control is something more than a matter of acquiring enough bargaining chips for our arms control negotiators. They are trying to teach something about the hard moral choices that currently confront us in the matter of nuclear weapons and strategic policy—not only those of us in the United States or its government, but all persons of good will everywhere.

Far from simplifying things, however, the Bishops have challenged us to choose among morally desirable goals, to decide among morally questionable means, and to wade through situations where the options can only be described as morally ambiguous. It is intentionally done.

As their letter states near the outset, "In all of this discussion of distinct choices, of course, we are referring to options open to individuals." We each have to make our own decisions about what is right in this matter. Together, 230 million of us will help shape American policy. In order for the collective policy to be morally acceptable, the individual contribution must be as thoughtful as it is honest.

If there is to be any success, it will come from many steps. In the meantime, we will continue to have the responsibility to protect the independence of our nation, and the freedoms that flourish here, from real enough threat. We must be loyal to our own liberty. And our freedom, whether we like it or not, is inextricably bound to the survival of the idea of a law of nations, and of kindred democratic societies in the Middle East and Asia no less than in Western Europe.

There was a catatonic quality to the decision to deploy the MX, an absence of will; a leakage of reality now passed the point of return. Within weeks it became known that the Pentagon had decided the next stage in nuclear defense would be the development and deployment of laser-beam satellites designed to destroy Soviet missiles in the booster stage, which is to say after launching. Each laser would be activated by a two-nuclear explosion. Now this is escape from reality; the mentality of the video arcade. But it, too, was in the 1980 Republican platform, which called for an "active defense" based in outer space. The proposed system would have the same function as that of the antiballistic-missile system, and the press routinely reported that its development would mark the formal abandonment of deterrence as American nuclear doctrine. The 1983 Defense appropriation provided $160 million to begin work on laser-related space defense. ("Boost phase intercept systems," as the term has emerged.) Mind, the Soviets have been hard at work developing more conventional radar-based missile defenses which, in the spirit of the ABM treaty, we have not done. We are merely taking the arms race into outer space.

We would be taking leave of our senses also, for there is only the remotest chance that even *one* of the satellites would work, much less a space armada of the same. (Consider the heavens churning in nuclear inferno, while all those little dials and digital devices go blithely about their doomsday detail.) Even so, the Soviet military will believe that we *will be able to bring it off.* Generally speaking, they think American technology can develop anything American science can discover (for example, the laser beam). If there is not much chance of the weapons actually working, neither is there much hope of maintaining the nuclear peace in such a race.

Nothing irreversible has yet happened. Nothing will until the first "Peacekeeper" is lowered into the first Minuteman silo, and that is some distance off in time yet. But already we see the fading of loyalties to principles that have been honorable and worked and have commanded our loyalties. After the MX vote, I spoke once again in the Senate, still pleading the case that we were making perhaps the most fatal mistake in our history. But I spoke to a body that could not remember what it was doing that was different.

It need not end this way. Loyalties can be revived— above all, the commitment to a guarded reasonableness, to that spirit which is never too sure it is right. A loyalty to the nation, but with an awareness that we set out to be an example to mankind, not a lesson to it.

T W O

АНТИСОВЕТИЗМ—

ПРОФЕССИЯ СИОНИСТОВ

Anti-Sovietism
Is the Profession
of Zionists

On July 1, 1982, the United States Permanent Representative to the United Nations, Jeane J. Kirkpatrick, was in Bujumbura, capital of Burundi, to represent the United States at the observance of the twenty-first anniversary of its independence. Life in the southern half of the former Belgian trust territory of Ruanda-Urundi had not been notably tranquil since 1962. The details from almanacs are spare but sufficient. The constitution was adopted in 1974, suspended in 1976. There is no legislative body. Rule is by the Supreme Revolutionary Council. Tribal warfare took more than 100,000 lives in 1972–73. Ninety percent of the population is illiterate. Enrollment in higher education in 1972 was 482. Money is short.

But for the national-day procession, funds were available for a colossal banner proclaiming, in French, "Zionism is Racism."

Nearer to home, that same summer a course was offered at the Stony Brook campus of the State University of New York entitled "The Politics of Race." One of the suggested topics for term papers was the proposition, "Zionism is as much racism as Nazism was racism." Evidently nothing vicious was intended; the professor involved was apparently familiar with the proposition, but not familiar enough to know what he was dealing with. He might (or might not) have had his curiosity aroused had he known that at just about the time students were registering for his course, a secret agreement was signed

(June 29, 1983) between the PARTIDO COMUNISTA DE CUBA / COMITE CENTRAL and THE NEW JEWEL MOVEMENT OF GRENADA in which the parties jointly undertook to carry on the struggle in the Caribbean "against imperialism, neo-colonialism, racism and Zionism."

This proposition dates, of course, from the resolution of the General Assembly of November 19, 1975, which declared "Zionism is a form of racism and racial discrimination." I was then our Permanent Representative, and have already written about that moment. I will pause only to describe two aspects of that day.

First, the vote was close. On an earlier procedural motion, when Belgium moved to adjourn debate, a good many African countries deserted the Soviet-Arab coalition that was driving the resolution through. On final passage the vote was 67 to 55, with 15 abstentions. Chaim Herzog, then the Israeli Permanent Representative and now President of Israel, later commented that this had been the highest pro-Israeli vote in a decade. It may prove the highest ever after. Events have only gotten worse since. Even so, the vote was decisive. An Orwellian coup had occurred at the United Nations, for so long the symbol of liberal expectations for the world. A peripeteia—that sudden reversal of circumstance in Greek drama—was now to be encountered on a larger scale. The language of totalitarianism had triumphed.

In some sense, the Zionism resolution might seem a pardonable surprise. The West, not just the United States, and not just Israel, had been working to prevent what at the time would have seemed a very great setback— the expulsion of Israel from the General Assembly. In this we succeeded. It might appear to ask too much that this seemingly makeshift, second-best response was not anticipated. In retrospect, I would argue the contrary.

To follow the argument, it is necessary to grasp the

role of ideological argument in the Soviet system. Where we would argue that events are willed by individuals, often acting in groups, Marxists must see scientifically demonstrable processes at work which are sufficiently understood to be predictable.

In Marxist-Leninist doctrine, the theory of nationalities is particularly important. If you accept that property relations are the fundamental determinants of social relations, then this becomes overriding and therefore attachments (like religious beliefs) are epiphenomcna, which should soon disappear under a Marxist-Leninist regime. Now of course they don't disappear. Ethnic identities and beliefs persist. Indeed, they steadily emerge as the single greatest threat to the internal unity of the Soviet Union and its hegemony over its empire. Witness Poland today. Many "nationalities" present this problem to the Great Russians in the Kremlin, and none more than the Jews.

Why are the Jews a threat? They are a significant internal minority and a people whose relatives have created a nation-state of their own, a state that is a bastion (yes, a military image) of Western influence in an area of great strategic significance to the Soviet Union. Israel, moreover, is a state largely founded by immigrants from Central Europe and Russia, and its very existence provides the best argument for the most conspicuous group of Soviet citizens who wish to leave that country.

Now, some trace of a primitive anti-Semitism may influence Soviet attitudes toward Israel. I wish neither to exaggerate nor to discount this. In the 1952 trial of Rudolph Slansky, then General Secretary of the Czechoslovak Communist party, charges of Zionist attachments were made. Slansky was a Jew. In the dock he pleaded to be punished for his "foul, rotten nature." Charles H. Fairbanks, Jr., judges that it was in 1952 "that 'Zionists' began to be used in the Soviet press as a codeword for Jews." The Slansky trial was the last such orgy of the Stalin era, as Stalin then died. But even as death approached, he was detecting a doctors' plot—doctors who were Jews. Yet, this cannot be the whole of it.

It was the 1967 war in the Middle East that raised the issue high on the Soviet agenda. Three events occurred. Israel overwhelmed its combined Arab neighbors, most of whom were armed by and clients of the Soviet Union. Second, the United States for the first time came to the aid of Israel in a military crisis. Henceforth, the Middle East was a setting in which Soviet arms would face American arms. Finally, the Israeli victory in the Six-Day War, as Bernard Lewis has written, "generated enormous enthusiasm among Soviet Jews." Zionism had proved itself in battle. In Moscow, "for the first time, Zionism was seen as a serious problem, comparable with other nationalist movements which had plagued the colonial administrators of Tsarist Russia and their Soviet successors." Even so, the first official reaction was merely to assert a linkage between "American imperialism" and the Israeli bourgeoisie. This required no doctrinal innovation.

At the outset of 1970, Israeli-Egyptian relations worsened. On February 12, the Israelis bombed a metal works near Cairo. There was talk of the United States providing Phantom jets for Israel; in that event, Egypt would want MIG-23s, probably with Russian pilots. Thereupon occurred the first Soviet response directed at the ideological basis of the Jewish state. On February 28, the Chief Rabbi of Moscow, Yehuda-Leib Levin, in an interview in *Izvestia*, the U.S.S.R. government newspaper, denounced Zionism as essentially an instrument of capitalists. The United States connection was made explicit. He said: "There is no doubt that in certain circles in the U.S.A., mainly among big capitalists and rich Jews, it would be disadvantageous if the Jewish workers in America knew the truth about the Soviet Union." Next, thirty-seven prominent Soviet intellectuals, including two Nobel Prize physicists, denounced the Israeli bombing, and March 2 was proclaimed a worldwide day of protest against Israeli aggression.

For reasons we cannot know, the following February the anti-Israel charges by the Soviets were brought to a wholly different level. Here we must contend with the terrible trauma of World War II. Apart from the Bolshevik revolution, and the several years of fighting that followed, the great travail of the Soviet system had been the war against Hitler. It was not a war they contrived. Indeed, in 1939 they had re-emerged on the international scene as the allies of Hitler in the partition of Poland. But then Hitler turned on them. The war that followed almost destroyed them. If it left the U.S.S.R. a greatly expanded power, it also left the Soviet people with an ineradicable memory of near defeat. Part of that memory involved pro-Nazi activities during World War II among Turkish, Iranian, and other Islamic peoples in the southern regions of the Soviet empire. After the war, these movements were frequently denounced by Soviet polemicists as "racist."

It is useful to keep in mind how new this word is. It does not appear in the *Oxford English Dictionary*, published in 1933. Evidently it first appears in English in a translation of Trotsky's *History of the Russian Revolution*, in a reference to the Pan-Slavic movements of the nineteenth century. It may indeed be a word of Russian origin! But after World War II, the Soviets used "racist" exclusively as an epithet directed to non-Slavic peoples suspected of foreign loyalties. It is easy enough to imagine how their propagandists might extend the term to

Zionism. (In the Soviet Union one is either a Russian or a Jew or another nationality. Identity cards so record.) Similarly, as Nazis were the model of a threat to the U.S.S.R., it may be comprehended how the Russians might come to compare Israeli behavior to Nazi behavior. But it is an amazing leap of invention to assert that Jews, far from being victims of the Nazis, had been their collaborators! And this now happened.

On February 18–19, 1971, a two-part article appeared in *Pravda*, and was promptly published as an English-language pamphlet, by Novosti Press Agency of Moscow, titled *Anti-Sovietism—Profession of Zionists*. In Russian, " АНТИСОВЕТИЗМ—ПРОФЕССИЯ СИОНИСТОВ ." The thirty-four-year-old author of the article was Vladimir Viktorovich Bolshakov, then (or shortly thereafter) Deputy Secretary of *Pravda*'s editorial board in charge of the newspaper's international department.

It would be interesting to know whether Bolshakov was the author of the idea as well as the article. It does *not* seem the sort of idea that would occur to a committee. But would it occur to this pedestrian, high-ranking, cautious propagandist? Bolshakov first came to Western notice with a 1967 article reproving George Kennan's view that political change will eventually come to the Soviet system, a proposition that was, of course, refuted by Lenin. He relates how the retired Ambassador, now said to be a part-time CIA agent, "rushed to Switzerland as the goldseekers once had rushed to California" to arrange the publication of Stalin's daughter's book, withal that "Alliluyeva was considerably more suited as an illustration of erosion of human decency and chasteness, than as confirmation of Kennan's theory of the erosion of the ideals of Communism in Russia."

Now, that is almost chatty, and, in truth, it does not take much invention to confirm Lenin's views in *Pravda*.

However, four years later Bolshakov had turned deadly serious and presented a proposition that has changed our times, literally. As mentioned earlier, he asserted in the official newspaper of the Communist party of the Soviet Union that Jews, far from being victims of the Nazis, had been their collaborators. "Zionist agents active during the last war in Western and Eastern Europe and in the occupied part of the Soviet Union, collaborated with the nazis. Many cases are known where Gestapo men recruited overseers for death camps and special 'police' from among Zionists who 'kept order' in Jewish ghettos. 'The tragedy of Babi Yar,' wrote a number of Soviet citizens of Jewish origin who live in the Ukraine, in a letter to *Pravda*, 'will forever be a reminder not only of the monstrous barbarity of the nazis but also of the indelible disgrace of their accomplices and followers—the Zionists.' " Zionists as accomplices of the Nazis! What lie could be more obscene?

This is the background of the Zionism resolution of the United Nations. It was a weapon waiting to be used, and its moment came in 1975 when another plan was thwarted. The irony was that this resolution, this second-best, fall-back alternative, was far more devastating to Israel than expulsion from the General Assembly would have been, for, in effect, the resolution denied legitimacy to the state of Israel. Again, it is a matter of the times. In the aftermath of colonialism, and not coincidentally in the context of the American civil-rights movement, racism was the one offense international society universally condemned.

Very well. We had been outfoxed. Even the Israelis had been caught off guard—Israelis who are *never* caught off guard. There was no occasion for blame. When the event did occur, the U.S. was anything but passive. The world knew our view. We had declared that we would not submit to a totalitarian lie. I spoke on the occasion: "The United States rises to declare before the General Assembly of the United Nations, and before the world, that it does not acknowledge, it will not abide by, it will never acquiesce in this infamous act."

This was the time for us to take the offensive. There was clear evidence, after several related votes, that the Soviets and the Arabs had overreached. Especially in sub-Saharan Africa, they could not command their usual majorities. The time was at hand for the United States, *and the West,* to make clear that we would be loyal to those who stood with us. There needed to be rewards and punishments, both concrete and avowed. The new nations in particular were learning their way in a new world and needed to have it made clear that there are matters the United States took with profound serious-ness—even if other nations do not.

And why? As one of the oldest governments on earth *we had learned the importance of elemental truth-telling and the appalling cost of official lies.* In 1975, there were nine nations in the world, eight of which were members of the United Nations, that had both existed in 1914 and not had their form of government changed by force since that date: United States, United King-dom, Australia, Canada, South Africa, New Zealand, Sweden, Liberia, and nonmember Switzerland. (The subsequent coup in Liberia reduced the number to eight.)

Yet having *said* No, we proceeded to give every pos-sible indication that we didn't really mean what we had said. The United Nations system works against moral seriousness. By this time, the European democracies had pretty much concluded that nothing important could happen there, and were disposed to think that taking the UN seriously showed a lack of sophistication. Moreover, they had little liking for Israel, the existence of which did in fact cause them inconvenience, if not indeed true difficulty. And so the first reaction was to whisper it about that the United States had somehow handled the matter badly. On November 20, ten days after the Zionism resolution was adopted, my wife was seated at a formal dinner next to Louis de Guiringaud, the Ambassador of France. The subject of the resolution arose. The eminent diplomatist (he was already an *Ambassadeur de France,* a rank reserved for five persons, and later became Foreign Secretary) explained that the vote would not have been lost if the United States's statement had not been so "confrontational." But the American statement—mine, quoted above—was made *after the vote.*

Having said No, we took no initiative. By contrast, the Soviets almost visibly came alive to what had fallen to them. Henceforth, condemnations of Israel in various UN forums routinely were cast in terms of the charges made against the Nazi leaders at the Nuremberg trials. Thus, in February 1976, the UN Commission on Human Rights found Israel guilty of "war crimes" in the occupied territories. Ever more assertively the images of condemnations drew on images from the fascist era. The term "Pretoria–Tel Aviv axis" made its appearance. In a pattern that became routine, the most advanced charges would first appear in the proceedings of one of the specialized agencies, such as UNESCO or the ILO, or at a special conference, such as that in Mexico City on International Women's Year. Next, the documents of the meeting would be "referenced" in some General Assembly or Security Council statement—an incomprehensible sequence of numbers, capital letters, and slashes. In the fullness of time, the words themselves would appear. A year less a day after the Zionism resolution, the

General Assembly, by 91 to 20, "strongly condemned" the collaboration of Israel with the racist regime of South Africa.

With the coming of the Carter administration a vast change occurred. A policy of "damage control" at the UN was replaced by one of engagement. Engagement, but *not* opposition. For practical purposes, the Carter diplomats took the view that if the majority of the General Assembly held some view, it must be right—or at least partially right. In the end, these men, speaking to delegates or to the world, helped to destroy their administration.

A defeat so overwhelming as that which Governor Reagan inflicted on President Carter soon takes on the air of the inevitable. But those who were defeated in no way looked upon the outcome as fated; to the contrary, the postelection view in the Carter White House was that things had been going well until March 1, 1980, when Ambassador Donald F. McHenry voted in favor of a particularly vicious anti-Israel resolution in the Security Council of the United Nations. Three weeks later, Secretary of State Cyrus R. Vance, before the Senate Foreign Relations Committee, refused to disavow the vote. Thereafter, everything spun out of control. The Carter people—some of them—left Washington convinced, and proclaiming, that defeat was brought on by malevolent incompetence at the U.S. Mission to the United Nations and the inability of the Secretary of State to control the Mission. What they did not proclaim, and only dimly understood, was that they themselves had put in place the ideas that helped bring them down; that, indeed, to an extent the outcome was fated.

As set forth by the President and others, the campaign sequence was as follows. Senator Edward M. Kennedy's challenge to Carter began poorly. On March

18, the two met in Illinois, the first industrial state to hold a primary. The President won handily. If Kennedy could be beaten a week later in New York, his candidacy would collapse. A private poll conducted by Dresner, Morris & Tortorello Research in late January and early February showed the President leading the Senator 54 percent to 28 percent among probable Democratic primary voters in New York, with only 13 percent undecided. Yet in the end, Kennedy won, 59 percent to 41 percent.

In a gracious gesture, after the results were in, then Lieutenant Governor Mario M. Cuomo, who had headed Carter's campaign in New York, called the President to apologize. "No," said Carter, as reported in *The New York Times,* "it was the United Nations vote."

For the March 1 resolution of the Security Council was not one merely "rebuking Israel on settlements in Arab-claimed territory"; it was a resolution by the highest body of the world political system that found Israel guilty of "flagrant violation" of the Fourth Geneva Convention. And what is the Fourth Geneva Convention? It is one of a series of treaties drawn up in the aftermath of the Nuremberg trials to codify the crimes of the Nazi regime and to make those crimes punishable under international law. The Fourth Geneva Convention addressed Nazi conduct in occupied territories, especially Poland. The Fourth Geneva Convention made Auschwitz a crime under international law. In the history of the Convention only one nation has ever been found guilty of violating it: Israel. The United States voted Aye. Bolshakov had triumphed.

One of the advantages of the Soviets at this time was Cuba having become head of the "Nonaligned Movement." In September 1979, the heads of state or government of eighty-nine of these countries met in Havana and issued a 130-page final declaration. The document presented a stark, Marxist, totalitarian, antidemocratic view of the world. Prior to the conference, the Cuban draft was circulated, and afterward it was reported that the draft had been moderated by the delegates. This was true with respect to Egypt (now a near-outcast for having signed the Camp David Accords), but not in the least with respect to Israel. Zionism was declared to be a crime against humanity. The nonaligned nations had come near to calling it a crime to be a Jew. Our government remained silent. (The draft Cuban article on Zionism and the final conference text were identical.)

The U.S. government knew what was going on; it knew that American no less than Israeli interests were involved. Or it should have known. The truth is it didn't want to know. To accept the Soviet strategy in all its detail and all its implications, and to accept the complacency with which others endorsed it, was to put in jeopardy too many other beliefs.

Now, it will be clear that there are many reasons why President Carter lost the election, of which the UN vote was only one, and scarcely the most important. What *is* important, however, is that the administration looked upon its United Nations record generally—the March 1980 vote aside—as a huge success. Other policies had failed, and that was understood. But UN policy was thought to have succeeded. When the fall of a President is involved, and just possibly the fall of his party, some notice should be taken. I fear that so long as the ideas underlying the Carter administration's UN policy are dominant within the Democratic party, Democrats will be out of power—and rightly so.

In normal circumstances, UN affairs play a marginal role in United States foreign policy, for the simple reason that American foreign policy is normally preoccupied with the Soviet Union, whereas the UN, with its profusion of small countries, even ministates, is the last setting in which two powers would wish to conduct their affairs. But to the incoming Carter administration, the attraction of the UN as a setting in which to conduct foreign policy was *precisely* the prominent role Third World Nations play in UN affairs. It was a setting in which the cold war could at last be put aside.

In his first major foreign policy address, President Carter reported that the United States had overcome its "inordinate fear of Communism," and proposed that the two powers now join in a cooperative effort to improve north-south relations, specifically through economic assistance to the developing nations. ("North-south" had become in United Nations usage a term denoting the affluent as against the poverty-stricken regions of the world.) The name of the UN Ambassador was elevated to second place on the directory of the State Department building, immediately below that of the Secretary.

Carter brought together two strains of Democratic thinking on foreign affairs. The first was the old tradition of liberal internationalism—the extension of domestic standards of social justice to the world at large—as exemplified by President Harry S. Truman's Point Four program and President John F. Kennedy's Alliance for Progress. The second was a newer strain of thought, one much at odds with the traditions of Truman and Kennedy. This was a view that had emerged in the course of the Vietnam War to the effect that the United States, by virtue of its enormous power, and in consequence of policies and perhaps even national characteristics that were anything *but* virtuous had indeed become a principal source of instability and injustice in the world. We were, in short, a status-quo power—and the status quo we were trying to preserve was intolerable. By contrast, a more positive future was available to mankind if it could break out of American dominion. For my part, the most evocative and excruciating memory of the onset of this point of view was the day in 1970 that a group of former Peace Corps volunteers, protesting the war, ran down the American flag at Peace Corps headquarters in Washington and ran up the Vietcong flag.

Through the 1970s, this view grew in strength within the Democratic party. It was most often to be encountered when issues of defense were involved. In 1980, R. James Woolsey, who served with distinction as Under Secretary of the Navy in the Carter administration, described how the agony of Vietnam had led many Democrats "to attack the *existence* of American military power as a way to curtail its exercise." Caution in the use of military power, indeed great caution, is one thing. Declining to possess it, in the face of a massively armed adversary, is another.

There was a corollary to this doctrine of self-denial in defense. It flowed from the idea that the political hostility the United States encountered around the world, especially in the Third World, was, very simply, evidence of American aggression or at least of American wrongdoing. The aggression could be military, but just as often it would be diagnosed as economic (the role of the multinational corporation), as ecological (plundering the planet to sustain an absurdly gross standard of living), or as ideological (asserting ideas of the past of no relevance to the future). Often this view would be presented as nothing more specific than not being "on the side of history" or "the side of change." No matter; the prescription was the same. If the United States denied itself the *means* of aggression, it would cease to be aggressive. When it ceased to be aggressive, there would be peace—in the halls of the United Nations no less than in the rice paddies of Southeast Asia.

As tanks and missiles are instruments of military aggression, so ideas are the means of diplomatic aggression, specifically, that array of attitudes, judgments, and prejudices which led Americans to suppose they represented, on balance, a successful society, one model of how developing societies, if fortunate, might turn out, and in the interval a fair standard by which to measure the merits of other societies.

Here, in the interest of what lawyers call full disclosure, let me acknowledge that, from the first, those members of the Carter administration responsible for policy at the UN—and more generally for relations with the developing nations—regarded my own brief tenure as U.S. Permanent Representative at the UN in 1975–76 as the prime example of American diplomatic aggression. This was the view of UN Ambassadors Andrew Young and Donald McHenry. In an interview published in September 1980, contrasting his performance with mine, McHenry said: "I don't believe in confrontation politics, I don't believe in name-calling. I do believe in communicating with them [i.e., Third World nations], in stating my views, listening to theirs, respecting their views, expecting them to respect mine." A few weeks later, on October 1, 1980, taking issue with a *New York Times Magazine* article by Bernard D. Nossiter titled "How the Third World Runs the UN," he returned to this theme: "The article was reminiscent of the speeches about the 'Tyranny of the Majority' that one of my predecessors used to deliver when he represented our country at what he later called 'A Very Dangerous Place.'"

It would be hard to pack more misinformation into a

single sentence. It was President Gerald R. Ford, in an address at the opening of the General Assembly in the fall of 1974, who warned the UN against "the tyranny of the majority." At the close of that session, Ambassador John A. Scali repeated the warning. If I ever used the phrase, which I do not recall doing, it was only to cite them. As for "A Very Dangerous Place," in 1978 I published a memoir titled *A Dangerous Place*. The first page related: "I had first gone to Washington with John F. Kennedy and then stayed on with Lyndon Johnson. There I learned as an adult what I had known as a child, which is that the world is a dangerous place—and learned also that not everyone knows this." My editor chose the phrase for the title, but it did not refer to the UN. As a seaman is taught about the sea, the UN is not inherently dangerous, but it is implacably punishing of carelessness.

Arrogance is yet a greater danger. And there is a certain arrogance in the view that the behavior of other nations is primarily responsive to the behavior of our own; that others act, not as autonomous societies, but as a kind of chorus responding to our signals. This was a delusion most accessible to those who, having opposed the war in Vietnam, saw the outcome as victory rather than defeat.

Following the election of 1968, I was asked by President-elect Richard M. Nixon to be his Assistant for Urban Affairs. I was then of the view—which I see no reason to change—that the Vietnam War had been lost and that only ruin could come from persisting in the effort to disengage in a manner that would permit a "decent interval" between our departure and the collapse of the regime in South Vietnam. On January 3, 1969, I wrote a long memorandum to Nixon, which included this passage: "Vietnam has been a domestic disaster. . . . As best I can discern the war was begun with the very highest of motives at the behest of men such as Mc-Namara, Bundy, and Rusk in a fairly consistent pursuit of post-war American policy of opposing Communist expansion and simultaneously encouraging political democracy and economic development in the nations on the Communist perimeter, and elsewhere for that matter. At the risk of seeming cynicism, I would argue that the war in Vietnam has become a disastrous mistake because we have lost it."

But the consequences of Vietnam, all the same, would have to be lived with, and adjusted to. Foremost among these would be a major opening for, and stimulus to, *Soviet* imperialism. Susan Sontag has acknowledged how little she and others in the antiwar movement had understood this equation: "It was not so clear to many of us as we talked of American imperialism how few options many of these countries had except for Soviet imperialism, which was maybe worse. When I was in Cuba and North Vietnam, it was not clear to me then that they would become Soviet satellites, but history has been very cruel and the options available to these countries were fewer than we had hoped. It's become a lot more complicated."

But the perception of such complexity was beyond the powers of the U.S. Mission to the UN under the Carter administration. Its members could not see the signs of a new phase of Soviet policy: military support for Ethiopia in 1977; coups in both Afghanistan and South Yemen in April 1978; the invasion of Cambodia in December 1978. Unable to explain all this, or to fit it to the purposes they had set themselves, American diplomats at the UN grew increasingly silent.

It also emerged that our representatives had little sense of the UN Charter as *law* that had to be upheld and expounded. A superb opportunity came in the fall of 1977 when the Soviets switched sides in the Horn of Africa, as war broke out in the Ogaden Desert, an ethnically Somali territory within Ethiopia. The Soviets actively entered the conflict on Ethiopia's side.

It happens that in 1975 the principal sponsor of the resolution that declared Zionism to be a form of racism was none other than Somalia, acting in its then capacity as an especially fawning satellite of the Soviets. Now its own time had come. The Somalis had started the war. Very likely they counted on Soviet support. Moscow judged Ethiopia more important. Of a sudden the Somalis were at our doors, begging for help, pleading for us to understand the "nature of the Soviet threat," Soviet "neocolonialism," the "Soviet plot to encircle the Gulf," the "Soviet contempt for human rights and the rights of small nations."

All true. When I rose to speak after the vote that November 10th, I had addressed my remarks specifically to the Somali delegation. I said, "Today we have drained the word 'racism' of its meaning. Tomorrow terms like 'national self-determination' and 'national honor' will be perverted in the same way to serve the purposes of conquest and exploitation. And when these claims begin to be made . . . it is the small nations of the world whose integrity will suffer."

Did Somalia suffer? To be sure. But at the hands of the Soviets. We, by contrast, were soon providing them aid. Nary a word said of its behavior in 1975. To persons whose deepest conviction was that Third World nations were hostile to the United States because of our own neocolonial behavior—whose strong disposition was to believe that the Soviet Union in almost all instances supported the true liberationist forces in the former colonial world while the United States, on the wrong side of history, backed brutal but doomed dictatorships—the events from 1977 to 1980 could make no sense. Whoever asked for our help deserved it.

During that period, President Carter achieved the Camp David Peace Accords. He was justifiably proud of having used patience and persuasion to end conflict between Israel and Egypt, the largest of the Islamic nations in the Middle East. But did not the Accords bring forth more hostility from the Third World—the "rejectionist front"—than had ever been evoked by the "confrontationist" policies of the past? To understand this, one had to entertain the possibility that the opposition we encountered there was *not* a matter of long-held grievances against our abuses of power. One had to entertain the possibility that there were those whose great fear was that, in seeking peace, we might succeed.

Confused, and after a point not altogether straightforward, the strategy of our diplomats in New York, backed up in the Department of State, underwent a subtle and disastrous transformation. They had begun with the proposition that if the United States put itself on the "right" side of history, we would find the nations of the world, most of which of course were "new," coming over to our side in turn. Unaccountably, however, they were still not on our side. To the contrary, some were actively seeking to undo the greatest diplomatic achievement the administration had to its credit, and no nation was objecting or trying to prevent them. Evidently, then, we must *still* be on the wrong side. Reasoning thus, our diplomats prepared themselves to vote for the Security Council resolution of March 1, 1980—and, although this was certainly not their intention, to help bring down the administration they served.

The chain of resolutions passed in condemnation of Israel by the Security Council in 1979–80 forms a complex story. Yet, to follow it, only a single point needs to be understood: As a direct result of American policy, the Security Council had been allowed to degenerate to the condition of the General Assembly. Under the UN Charter, the General Assembly reaches decisions by majority vote, but its decisions are purely advisory or recommendatory (Article 10). By contrast, the Security Council has power. In situations where it determines that there is a "threat to the peace, breach of the peace, or act of aggression," the Security Council "shall make recommendations or decide what measures shall be taken. . . ." These included "such action by air, sea, or land forces as may be necessary. . . ."

The Security Council, in a word, may make war. And for that reason the Security Council does not operate by majority vote. Any permanent member may veto any action, simply by voting No. However, in the face of the increasingly vicious Soviet-Arab assaults that followed Camp David, the United States began to "abstain." I have represented the United States on the Security Council; I have served as President of the Security Council. *I state as a matter of plain and universally understood fact that for the United States to abstain on a Security Council resolution concerning Israel is the equivalent of acquiescing.*

The March 1 vote, when we voted against Israel, rather than merely abstaining, was a disaster, and it should have stimulated a reappraisal of the route by which the administration had traveled to it. Israel had been permanently damaged, and (unless their perceptions are perilously dulled) other allies of the United States had been permanently warned. Yet no more was said than that it was a mistake, and only a partial mistake at that. The Carter administration had failed in its objective at the UN; but to admit that failure was to cast in doubt the view of the world that justified the objectives. To avoid having to face this dilemma, the administration began to undermine the Camp David Accords—its one great success. They never thought their way through the matter.

An epilogue of sorts took place in the third week of December 1980, as the Carter administration and the 35th General Assembly began winding down. On Monday, December 15, the General Assembly adopted five resolutions on the Middle East more virulent and anti-Semitic than anything the UN had yet seen. The debate was obscene. Thus the Ambassador from Jordan speaking of the Ambassador from Israel: "The representative of the Zionist entity is evidently incapable of concealing his deep-seated hatred toward the Arab world for having broken loose from the notorious exploitation of its natural resources, long held in bondage and plundered by his own people's cabal, which controls and manipulates and exploits the rest of humanity by controlling the money and wealth of the world." The occasion for this diatribe was the receipt of the most recent Report of the Committee on the Exercise of the Inalienable Rights of the Palestinian People, a body established by a General Assembly resolution on November 10, 1975, the same day Zionism was declared to be a form of "racism and racial discrimination." The first of the resolutions was breathtaking: "Security Council Resolution 242 of 22 November 1967 does not provide an adequate basis for a just solution for the question of Palestine."

Resolution 242, of 1967, guaranteeing the right of nations in the Middle East to live in peace with "secure and recognized boundaries," is the one, the *single*, international guarantee of Israel's right to exist. In one form or another, that right had now been under constant assault for over five years. The nation was criminal; the nation was illegal; its capital was the occupied territory of other peoples. (By 1983, a summit conference of non-aligned nations would assert that even "West Jerusalem" was occupied Arab territory, including the Knesset, the holocaust memorial, and the President's house.) Now the General Assembly proposed to withdraw the one unqualified international title to which Israel could lay claim, the guarantee of Resolution 242. The United States said nothing. *No American delegate went to the podium to offer the least demur.* The campaign continued. On November 16, 1983, seven years and six days from the moment when as Israeli Permanent Representative he stood at the podium of the UN General Assembly and tore in two the resolution proclaiming Zionism to be a form of racism, Chaim Herzog returned, this time as President of his country. He came in peace. "Let us begin to talk," he said. "Let us forget the bitterness of the past." Half the membership of the UN either was not present, or walked out. As he was introduced to the General Assembly the Permanent Representative from Iraq objected on the ground that, according to United Nations resolutions, Israel's claim that Jerusalem was its capital "null and void." The poison was working.

One of the most dishonest (and debilitating, because profoundly misleading) assertions of the U.S. Mission during the Carter years was that the 1975 Zionism resolution was somehow brought about by the United States. Having resisted, America was now judged to have provoked. *That* resolution, on the key procedural motion, mustered a 67 to 55 majority, with 15 abstentions. *This* resolution, potentially far more destructive, was adopted 98 to 16, with 32 abstentions.

There was something to note about the sponsors of the resolutions. The familiar Soviet-leaning or Soviet-dominated nations were present: Afghanistan, Cuba, Laos

People's Democratic Republic. But also present were Nicaragua and Zimbabwe, two Third World nations with which the Carter administration had presumably established relations of friendship and respect.

In an editorial titled "Joining the Jackals," *The Washington Post* (which had supported the President for reelection) described this American vote against Israel in the Security Council on that Friday as representative of "the essential Carter." Now the President himself was being held to account. American failure was total. And it was squalid. These men, in both New York and Washington, helped to destroy the President who had appointed them and they deeply injured the President's party. They hurt the United States and they hurt nations that have stood with the United States in seeking something like, or near to, peace in the Middle East. They came to office full of themselves but empty of a steady understanding of the world. The world was a more dangerous place when at last they went away.

Later, on October 20, 1983, the General Assembly by a vote of 79 to 43 with 19 abstentions decided not to take up the issue of expelling Israel from the United Nations. The representative of the Palestine Liberation Organization thereupon criticized the Assembly for the decision. In his statement, made from the floor of the Assembly, where he has observer status, he referred to Israel as the "Judeo-Nazi regime in Tel Aviv" and told the delegates "you are perpetuating Hitlerian doctrine in this Assembly."

At the risk of being called an alarmist, I would again argue that a sustained ideological struggle is under way in the world. The forces of liberalism are under incessant attack—an attack that the West somehow avoids knowing about. The phase during which this assault was directed almost exclusively at Zionism and at Israel as a metaphor for democracy is now about over. A more general case against democracy is being made. A British friend, wise in the ways of that world, put it thus: "They are now on Page 16 of The Plan." What terrors impel the attack? What loyalties will resist it? The answers are needed because the questions will not go away.

THREE

The Idea of
Law in the
Conduct of
Nations

For a number of years I served as United States Ambassador to India, where I came to know a fair number of Peace Corpsmen. The program wasn't all that helpful to the Indians—the Indian government, at considerable cost, felt obliged to keep them under constant surveillance. We all understood this mild paranoia as the program was phasing out. My concern was that the young men and women leave in good order, feeling they'd done their best and realizing that they themselves, at least, had probably learned more than they'd taught. The problem with my plan was that it was continuously being interrupted by medical emergencies.

This problem lay with the Rule. The Rule was, of course, Never Drink the Water. Yet sooner or later everyone did. The day would be scorching, the temptation overwhelming, the flesh weak. At this point, the personalities I came to think of as Calvinist would quite collapse. Having found themselves capable of sin, they would judge themselves doomed and commence to sin with abandon. Almost invariably, this brought about the doom considered predestined. By contrast, gentler souls occasionally fell into sin, but more or less readily extricated themselves—sustained by their conviction that, after all, no one is perfect, one can but try. This meant most of them escaped harm, for it is not drinking the water *once* that brings certain ruin, but drinking it regularly. Then, the odds are overwhelming.

More and more, one finds that "Calvinist" sense of lost

innocence and the necessary, consequential degradation in the conduct of American foreign policy. In February 1980, I wrote in *The New Republic* that I genuinely feared the Carter administration would "turn out looking like the third act of *Rain,* with no sense of principle left intact." I believe that this did happen. The next administration came on the scene proclaiming that, inasmuch as the Soviets dissemble and cheat and Lord knows what else, they were going to get a taste of their own medicine. In the pursuit of truth and justice, it was prepared to do *anything* to oppose Communism.

In the Carter administration's first serious crisis with the Soviet Union, the invasion of Afghanistan in 1979, the President was evidently disoriented by the discovery that the Soviet leader had deceived him. On December 31, 1979, he told Frank Reynolds of ABC that, in a message explaining the Afghan invasion, Mr. Brezhnev had simply lied. The President also said: "This action of the Soviets has made a more dramatic change in my own opinion of what the Soviets' ultimate goals are than anything they've done in the previous time I've been in office." In all fairness, he tried to do something—imposing a grain embargo and withdrawing from the Moscow Olympics—but the response was more one of disillusion than of principle. It was intensely personal. He had been lied to by a man he had hugged and kissed when they'd last met.

That the Soviets had grievously violated international law was not the ground on which we acted. It ought to have been. Disillusion disappears with the disillusioned. The grain embargo, in a sense, lasted until the Iowa Republican caucuses a few months later, when Ronald Reagan renounced the whole undertaking.

The fact was, the Soviets had taken Afghanistan. It

was idle to think that they would pull out and agree to some neutral status. The Russian/Soviet pattern is consistent. Writing of a trip through Czarist Central Asia in 1888, Lord Curzon, who later became Viceroy of India, said: "A conviction of the permanence of Russian conquests is . . . [an] important element in explaining the bases of her power. A forward movement, whether voluntarily undertaken or beneath the pressure of circumstances, is seldom repented of and never receded from."

For the United States and other nations concerned, the only practical response to the Soviet act was to assert that traditional international law *and* the United Nations Charter had been violated in a manner that admitted of no statute of limitations. Our embassy should have been closed in Kabul on grounds that now there was no legitimate Afghan government; and an office should have been opened in the State Department that would press the legal issue in every possible forum for as long as the occupation persisted. True, this would be a long time: but as a nation we expect to be around a long time. Our response to the Soviet occupation of Latvia, Lithuania, and Estonia in 1940 was never to accept the *fait accompli*. We reacted then as to a violation of law. This is no longer our reaction. One asks: If Leonid Brezhnev *had* told the truth, what *would* Jimmy Carter have done?

President Reagan's first crisis with the Soviet Union came on August 31, 1983, when a Soviet interceptor plane shot down a Korean 747 airliner on a scheduled flight from New York to Seoul. This time the Presidential response was even more disoriented. On September 7, in *The Washington Post,* Edwin M. Yoder, Jr., said: "Not, perhaps, since Teddy Roosevelt tongue-lashed 'the bandits in Bogota,' has the world heard a president speak as harshly of another regime as did Ronald Reagan in his first reaction to the destruction of the Korean airliner. It was, he said, 'a terrorist act' about which the Soviet government had 'flagrantly' lied."

Indeed, the language soon grew even harsher. "Massacre" was one of the milder terms. Yet the President *did nothing*. Grain sales went forward, releasing Soviet resources for the production of oil and gas, thereby increasing their hard currency earnings, machinery was shipped, a vast conference at Madrid agreed that progress in human rights was being made by all the signatories of the Helsinki Accords. William Safire, normally a supporter of Reagan, was appalled: "A U.S. President, in response to the Soviet massacre of sixty-one U.S. citizens traveling under the protection of U.S. passports, has sounded off more fiercely than Theodore Roosevelt and has acted more pusillanimously than Jimmy Carter."

Soon Reagan was being praised for his restraint and statesmanship. But ought he to have been? To act in such a manner invites contempt from the leaders of the Soviet Union; and nothing is more dangerous in so powerful an adversary. On the other hand, it is not difficult to discern the sources of his inaction. The United States did not approach the incident as a violation of a treaty, specifically the Chicago Civil Aviation Convention of 1944, to which the Soviet Union is a signatory. Article 9 of the treaty required the Soviets to help the lost plane, not to shoot it down. The incident, although horrifying, was, even so, limited. (The invasion of Afghanistan was a vastly more grievous offense against world order.) The role of law in every civilization is to provide a proportionate response to the violation of a norm. Absent the role of law, aggrieved nations either do nothing or go to war. This was Reagan's dilemma. Thinking and speaking in emotional, moralistic terms, he had to realize that if he did *anything* it could easily be taken as the first step toward a warlike policy. Having made military strength with respect to the Soviets the centerpiece of his foreign policy, he now found himself immobilized for fear that his acts would be taken as a prelude to using that strength. On September 9, 1983, the President spoke his mind, asking plaintively, "Short of going to war, what would they have us do?"

Similarly, in a news conference October 19, 1983, Reagan said of the activities of the Central Intelligence Agency, "I do believe in the right of a country when it believes that its interests are best served to practice covert activity. . . ." This, again, is a wholly normless statement. A nation has such a right if it is *in* the right—which is to say, if its behavior is consonant with international law. Given the behavior of the Nicaraguan government toward at least one of its neighbors, there is, I believe, a right of action there. But if the President should decide to bring about the partition of Canada, he would have no right whatever to begin shipping arms to dissidents in Quebec. Is this such a difficult distinction for a President to make, or does it represent the gradual evanescence of the idea of law in international affairs? James Reston spotted the remark immediately. "Mr. Reagan," he wrote, "has a way of saying what he truly believes in news conferences, which may be why he has so few of them." Fair enough: the President had indeed said what the Soviets believe. The Sovietization of American foreign and military policies proceeds. But did he say it out of a changed belief, or a vanished one? I would contend the latter. The world view of a Woodrow Wilson or a Franklin D. Roosevelt was simply no longer accessible to a President not trained to the task. In 1922, John H. Clarke resigned from the Supreme Court in order to serve as head of the League of Nations Non-Partisan Associ-

ation, promoting the cause of American adherence to a
system of world order and world law. He had been appointed by Woodrow Wilson and felt that loyalty to Wilson's ideals required this of him. But what would an
American President in the 1980s know of such loyalties?

I do not mean to criticize the President personally. I
speak of that institutional state of mind which, having
lost the principle of proportionality basic to all law, can
think of no option as between doing nothing, or next to
nothing, and blowing up the world. Freud is said to have
remarked that the first man who cursed an enemy rather
than striking him was the founder of civilization; just so
with the first nation that instead of "going to war" thought
of going to court.

In an address given in February 1979, I took as my
central theme "the proposition that the current disori-
entation in American foreign policy derives from our
having abandoned, for all practical purposes, the concept that international relations (and also to a degree the
internal conduct of governments) can and should be
governed by a regime of public international law. Further, this idea has not yet been succeeded by some other
reasonably comprehensive and coherent notion as to the
kind of world order we *do* seek, or which at all events
we do accept and try to cope with." I said this to the
Council on Foreign Relations. One would have assumed
a sympathetic audience for such a theme in such a setting. In the event, the reaction was the opposite. If de-
fenestration were practiced at the Harold Pratt House on
Park Avenue, I would have been done for. Feelings are
aroused by this issue for reasons I do not understand.
Withal, I press the case.

Neither the Carter administration then nor the Reagan administration now display a sense of the past

American commitment to the role—if not the *rule*—of law in world affairs. I refer, in the first instance, to that vision associated in the American mind primarily with President Woodrow Wilson. It is useful to keep in mind that no man in the history of the world—certainly no other in our century—so engaged the passions and the hopes of mankind as Wilson did in those decisive months of 1918 and 1919. In huts in Poland, Hungary, Yugoslavia, his name was spoken with reverence and even his picture was treasured.

The idea that a world ruled by law would be an ideal one is as old, almost, as the idea of law itself. But only in the latter part of the nineteenth century did it come to be seen as a practical vision, and a reasonable choice that governments might make in determining their own behavior. It is probably fair to say that at the turn of the twentieth century most statesmen in the West believed in such a possibility for the world. It was part of the prevailing optimism and was based in part on the confident expectation that liberal democracy—with its great emphasis on law as the arbiter of relations among citizens with equal rights—would become a near-to-universal form of government.

To be sure, the literature of international law was primarily European until recently—the term itself is the invention of a European, Jeremy Bentham. At the turn of the century it was European statesmen who were most prominently associated with the idea of establishing mechanisms for the pacific settlement of international disputes. The Czar of Russia called into being the Hague Peace Conference of 1899, which established the Permanent Court of Arbitration, or the Hague Tribunal, as it is more generally known. But the second Hague Conference, which met in 1907, was proposed by Theodore Roosevelt, who had received the Nobel Peace Prize for his successful efforts to bring to a close the then recent Russo-Japanese war. If the idea of setting up arrangements for the "peaceful settlement of disputes" became a vogue in Europe, it became something of an obsession in the United States.

In his fine biography of William Jennings Bryan, Louis W. Koenig describes the luncheon at which Wilson, as President-elect, offered the post of Secretary of State to the great commoner. Bryan had one concern and one condition. His concern was that he and his wife, Mary, objected to the serving of intoxicating liquors at their table, which might prove embarrassing at state functions. Wilson responded that this was a matter on which they could feel perfectly free to follow their own wishes. Bryan's *condition* was that "he be allowed to negotiate a series of peace treaties in accord with a draft that he produced, a typewritten version of a model treaty." Wilson read the draft and said he had no objection. Bryan said this was not enough. He wanted to be sure of Wilson's willingness to press for the treaties, that they be, in Koenig's words, "an integral part of his foreign policy." Wilson agreed; Bryan accepted on the spot. Wilson himself insisted on filling the post of Counselor to the State Department (which is to say, the chief legal adviser) with John Bassett Moore, of Columbia University, the most distinguished professor of international law of the time.

It is all well and good to make light of Bryan, a pacifist Secretary of State in a world heading into the greatest war ever known. He negotiated thirty treaties for the Advancement of Peace, each setting up procedures for conciliation to be put in place promptly, with named conciliators, so as to be ready when needed. The first was with El Salvador—no great feat, given the atmosphere of the time—but others were with France, Britain, and Italy. In the end, twenty were ratified and promulgated. Was all this a bit naïve? Yes. But was not the war that came utter, sheer, irreversible madness? Yes, also.

There were achievements. Some of the damage Theodore Roosevelt had done in Central America was undone. Colombia was paid an indemnity for Panama and was offered an apology. In truth, Wilson was a bit trigger happy in the Caribbean and even tried, unsuccessfully, to persuade the Senate to make a protectorate of Nicaragua. (Banks were about to place that country in receivership.) But the idea of law persisted, even when it did not prevail.

Bryan emerges as the first advocate of a policy of restraint that others were to embrace, if not always to abide by, for the rest of this century. He resigned over the note sent to Germany after the sinking of the *Lusitania* off the Irish coast on May 7, 1915. He wanted to mediate. Wilson wanted the Germans to abide by the law of the sea. These were compatible positions, but not to men of such different disposition. Step by step, Wilson took the nation into war on grounds that international law left no recourse.

With the war ended, the President proposed the establishment of a world organization which through the enforcement of law would prevent such a war from ever again happening. The organization—the League of Nations—was created, even as its sustaining vision was shattered. I refer to the great collapse of confidence in human progress that resulted from violence on a scale never before known. It was a convulsion beyond the grasp of any merely political mind. William Butler Yeats went to the heart of it in his poem "The Second Coming," lines that haunt our minds to this day as final, awful prophesy:

> Things fall apart; the centre cannot hold;
> Mere anarchy is loosed upon the world, . . .

But there was a political event as well: the establishment in Russia of the first totalitarian state, with a government wholly rejecting Wilsonian beliefs and principles, law not least, as epiphenomena of a soon-to-vanish economic system.

The United States did not join the League; but the idea of law as the arbiter of international relations was scarcely abandoned here. The American government, with unsuspected vigor and unequaled confidence, set about drafting and obtaining ratification of treaties limiting arms and renouncing violence. The conviction that the United States *must* join the Permanent Court of International Justice persisted through Republican and Democratic administrations alike, and for two decades engaged the energies of the leaders of the American bar.

It fell to Franklin D. Roosevelt, who had been Assistant Secretary of the Navy during World War I, to bring Wilson's vision to fulfillment a generation later. Roosevelt had been more than a passive onlooker in 1919. The Treaty of Versailles provided that the first International Labor Conference, of the new International Labor Organization, was to meet in Washington in January of that year. The delegates and the small secretariat arrived to find President Wilson in a coma and the Senate deadlocked in debate over the treaty. To the astonishment of at least the British, who couldn't imagine a "junior minister" daring to do such a thing, Roosevelt emptied a temporary Navy building on the Mall of its admirals and turned it over to the ILO secretariat. On becoming President himself, he moved directly toward affiliation with the ILO, which the United States joined in 1934. It would appear he was also moving in the direction of joining the League of Nations.

Well before World War II was over, Roosevelt put in place the planning for a new world organization, taking the greatest care to avoid Wilson's mistakes, especially in dealing with the United States Senate. (He did not, however, take great care of himself, and was dead before the United Nations came into being. When Wilson was a professor, he watched as Bryan launched the first Presidential campaign—far less strenuous then than now—and wrote that no normal person could stand that pace. The nation would henceforth be reduced to choosing its chief magistrates from among "wise and prudent athletes, a small class.")

Had Roosevelt lived, the UN might have got off to a better start, but it is hard to think just how. True, the Soviets insisted on great-power rights, such that the "new" world started out with unequal classes of nations. (But, in terms of power, the nations *were* unequal, and would become even more so as a great range of former colonies came to independence and membership.) But note, the Soviet insistence on three votes in the General Assembly—for the Soviet Union itself, the Byelorussia S.S.R., and the Ukrainian S.S.R. Evidently, they thought they would need the votes to offset the British Empire in closely contested issues with important outcomes. In the proceedings of the San Francisco conference of 1945, at which the UN was formally established, it seemed that a more experienced and perhaps more practical Wilsonianism was in place, its ideals somehow vindicated by the devastation of the war, which was seen to have been the consequence of the unwillingness of the democracies to defend those ideals.

It seems so long ago, so remote, indeed, as to make it

scarcely possible to invoke those days as an experience that makes any claim on our present behavior. Yet it is the case that, at first, we took our obligations under the Charter with profound seriousness—and expected others to do so as well. In 1946, when the United States alone possessed the atomic bomb, we offered to turn it over to the United Nations for the purpose of maintaining world peace, which is to say, to use the powers of government to obtain compliance with law. This was the famous "Baruch Plan."

And when, in 1950, North Korea invaded its neighbor to the south, the United Nations directed that the aggression be repulsed, and under United Nations banners this was done by an armed force made up of contingents from fourteen countries. In 1956, when the Soviet Union sent its forces into Hungary, the General Assembly voted to "condemn the violation of the Charter . . . by the Union of Soviet Socialist Republics in depriving Hungary of its liberty and independence, and the Hungarian people of the exercise of their fundamental rights."

Note the reference to the "fundamental rights" of the Hungarian people. The Charter imposes a dual obligation on governments. They are to be law-abiding in their relations with one another, *and also with their citizens*. The textual parallels with the United States Constitution are obvious and were deliberate. The Constitution begins "We the people of the United States . . ." The Charter begins "We the peoples of the United Nations. . . ."

The Charter commits governments to honor "fundamental human rights" as these were understood by British and American constitutional lawyers in 1944. Others understood this, and made use of that understanding for their own purposes. In 1946, Spain applied for membership. Poland blocked its application, arguing that Spain was not a democracy, because it did not have free elections, and was accordingly ineligible for membership until its internal arrangements were put in proper order.

The Charter of the Organization of American States, signed in Bogotá in 1948, similarly presumes that member governments will be democratic in character. The OAS was the first of the regional organizations envisioned in the UN Charter, and it modeled itself after that parent. The preamble asserts that the nations of North and South America are "confident that the true significance of American solidarity and good neighborliness can only mean the consolidation on this continent, *within the framework of democratic institutions*, of a system of individual liberty and social justice based on respect for the essential rights of man" (emphasis added).

All this seems far away, as if it were some scheme for universal improvement that Bryan had dreamed up. Yet it happened. Then things fell apart. Why? Simply put, the United Nations was not able to deal with totalitarian forces any more than was the League. Antidemocratic forces managed to gain effective control of the organization. This is in sharp contrast to the experience of the League of Nations, which, if impotent in the face of fascist and Communist regimes, was at least never dominated by them. Germany left the League in 1933 over disarmament, and the Soviet Union was expelled in 1939 over Finland.

The UN experience—and by extension the experience of this past generation—has also been shaped by, and in turn has helped to reinforce, the peculiar difficulties the liberal democracies have found in dealing with rhetoric of the totalitarian left. It is useful to recall that there was, at first, some problem in recognizing the realities of fascism and Nazism. But these *were* recognized after a relatively short period because the purposes of the totalitarian right were too assertively illiberal. In contrast, the totalitarian left, by adopting and distorting the language of liberalism in the manner we have come to know as Orwellian, has blunted perceptions within the democracies. As a result, a huge transmutation in an organization such as the United Nations could take place without any very clear recognition by a government, or even public opinion, that something extraordinary had occurred.

Alarms were raised, as they frequently are, by writers. As early as the 1950s, Hans J. Morgenthau was asserting the de facto primacy of national interests in the behavior of governments that left little room for the normative considerations that are presumably embodied in law. "Whether or not a nation shall pursue a policy of alliances," he wrote in 1959, "is, then, not a matter of principle but of expediency."

Then, with the Vietnam War, there came about a great falling off of confidence in those normative standards as such. Vietnam, as William Pfaff has written, was "liberalism's war." Opposition to it, very simply, brought opposition to liberalism, or at least to the notion of its universal applicability, a notion implicit in the League of Nations, the United Nations, and the Organization of American States. Think of George Kennan, who is so much associated with the postwar foreign policy of "containing" Soviet expansion—in the name of which the United States has fought two hard and costly wars.

In a 1976 interview published in *Encounter*, Kennan called for "withdrawal from our far-flung foreign involvements" for the simple and central reason that "we have nothing to teach the world." We had no answers to the "problems of human society in the modern age." Even if we did, answers appropriate to our problems would have no relevance to those of other societies, for ours was different from all other societies. He "emphatically rejected the concept of the universality of the American experience." What might be possible here, with our wealth and innocence, is simply not possible elsewhere. And that is all there is to say.

In sum: Wilsonian thinking had already got us into sufficient trouble; it could only get us into worse. It may be that this is an oversimplification of Kennan's thesis, but it is a view increasingly held by Americans generally. In 1983, the Chicago Council on Foreign Relations published the results of a nationwide survey of attitudes regarding this nation's role in the world. The results indicate a "continuing erosion of the post-World War II public consensus that the national interest requires active participation by the United States in world affairs. Only a bare majority of the public now holds the opinion that such international activism is best for the future of the country, while over a third now say that it would be better if the United States 'stayed out' of world affairs."

This is in part, of course, an aspect of a renascent economic nationalism born of hard times. It seems to indicate that sustained American prosperity will be achieved if only we can put a bit of distance between our own and the world's economy. It derives also, I submit, from wide acceptance of Kennan's lament that the United States of America is more of an aberration in the world than a model for it. Where once, in Daniel Bell's words, there was "a well-nigh universal expectation that the United States would inherit the future," there is now a growing feeling that the American experience is irrelevant or unnecessary to most of the rest of the world.

In June 1982, President Reagan delivered an exceptional and moving address to the British Parliament in which he revealed his administration's intention to sponsor a program fostering democratic institutions around the world. "Project Democracy," it came to be called. Two days after the President's speech, the former Under Secretary of State George W. Ball, widely and properly regarded as an *éminence grise* of American diplomacy, remarked, "crusade for democracy . . . I thought we had gotten over that a long time ago."

Then, in January 1979, the UN Security Council took up the matter of the Soviet-backed Vietnamese invasion of Cambodia. The Czechoslovak and Soviet representatives on the Security Council simply flat-out denied there had been any such invasion, asserting that there had been an internal uprising over which the Security Council had no jurisdiction. It was a straight-faced totalitarian lie, but an altogether predictable one. A Soviet veto put an end to any prospect even of censure. And in contrast to 1956, when the Soviets had invaded Hungary, there was no action by the General Assembly.

In December 1979, the Soviets invaded Afghanistan. This time a General Assembly resolution was passed, in January of 1980, although the Assembly dared not mention the Soviets by name. Rather, the resolution called for "immediate, unconditional and total withdrawal of the foreign troops from Afghanistan. . . ." In three subsequent General Assembly resolutions (adopted in the fall of 1980, 1981, and 1982), the words "unconditional and total" disappeared; the Soviet Union continued unmentioned.

There are several things to learn here. One is that nations denounce other nations from which they have nothing to fear. The United States is routinely denounced as a threat to world peace in the declarations and communiqués of the so-called nonaligned countries. The Soviets are seldom mentioned, never condemned. If you would know who is feared, note who is not denounced. Another lesson is that the United Nations treatment of the Soviet invasion of Afghanistan not only did not surprise us, but was in fact expected. Increasingly, the United States responds to such violations of the Charter—and, by extension, to the regime of traditional international law on which the Charter was based—not in terms of law and legal obligations, but in terms of a narrow and almost normless realpolitik.

During my tenure as U.S. Permanent Representative to the UN, Spanish Sahara was partitioned by Morocco and Mauritania, and Portuguese Timor was invaded and conquered by Indonesia. In both instances the United States was more than content that this should happen, while the Soviet Union, in one instance, and the People's Republic of China, in the other, very much tried to prevent it. The notion of law no more entered *our* policy considerations than it did *theirs*.

The overrunning of Spanish Sahara was especially poignant, as, a year earlier, the African nations, fearing Spain might not give up its colony, had called on the International Court of Justice for an advisory opinion, which, delivered only weeks before the partition and occupation of the territory by two African neighbors, ringingly asserted the right of the people of that colony to freedom and independence.

To say again, it may be that American opinion is moving away from an era in which we set great store by customary international law and expected fruitful development of treaty law, which would result in a comprehensive body of rules that would govern the conduct of nations. There has been a perhaps related decline in religious belief: an experience not typically offset by the adoption of a comprehensive set of alternative beliefs. In politics, there is always as Wordsworth described it:

> The good old rule
> . . . the simple plan,
> That they should take, who have the power,
> And they should keep who can.

Americans would not like to think that their country's foreign policy was based on such principles. If, clearly, at times it is, it is not yet because we wish it so.

Manifestly, we cannot hold the rest of the world to a good many of the propositions relating to their internal conduct that we wrote into covenants and charters and declarations with such earnestness in the first half of this century. An ancient doctrine (going back at least to Grotius) is *rebus sic stantibus,* which denotes "a tacit condition, said to attach to all treaties, that they shall cease to be obligatory as soon as the state of facts and conditions upon which they were founded has substantially changed" *(Black's Law Dictionary).* For all that Chapter II of the charter of the Organization of American States requires of members "the effective exercises of representative democracy," this is not going to be the political norm of this hemisphere or this world during the foreseeable future. It had once looked that way; it no longer does. Circumstances have changed. What has not changed—what the United States must strive to make clear has not changed—is the first rule of international law: *Pacta sunt servanda,* agreements must be kept.

Consider the matter of human rights. This was a bold extension of Western, liberal ideas into the field of international law, a subject that from its beginnings was thought to be concerned essentially with the rights and obligations of nations. The largest single initiative was the creation of the International Labor Organization. The working mode of the ILO was to draft conventions and treaties that spelled out certain rights to which working men and women were entitled, and which the signatory nations undertook to guarantee and protect. The original theory of labor treaties rested on the economists' concept of innovator costs. If Belgium enacted legislation mandating an eight-hour day or forbidding night work for women, its labor costs would presumedly increase and its industries would be at a competitive disadvantage with those, let us say, of France. If both nations were to adopt the same standards simultaneously, and in the company of all the principal industrial nations, no innovator cost would be incurred, and nations which, for the most part, wanted to do these things would be free to.

Labor treaties proved to be a clumsy idea. Generally speaking, the lower a nation's actual labor standards the more labor treaties it will have signed. (The United States agreed only to a limited number of maritime conventions, that being a clear area of jurisdiction of the federal government.) On the other hand, the ILO proved a durable institution. It was surely the one organization of the League of Nations the United States would have been thought least likely to join, yet it was the one we did join. The reason we did, and the reason the institution has endured, is the support given by the free trade unions of the world. It has raised to the level of international treaty law a number of principles of great importance to them. Of these, none is more important than the right to organize and bargain collectively. It took thirty years for this right to be incorporated in a labor treaty, thirty years of serious, sustained advocacy, which finally prevailed. In 1948, the International Labor Conference adopted the Freedom of Association and Protection of the Right to Organize Convention. It took force in 1950. As of 1983, ninety-four countries had ratified it, including the Soviet Union, the Communist nations of Eastern

Europe, and China. In 1949, the Right to Organise and the Collective Bargaining Convention was adopted, strengthening the earlier document. It went into force in 1951, and has been ratified by 110 countries.

Now, it is the plain and painful fact that no more than half the signatories to labor treaties in fact do abide by them. Some nations saw in them a kind of standard they agreed to aspire to, and perhaps someday attain. Others, such as Czechoslovakia, faithfully adhered to the convention until totalitarian regimes came to power. That is the world we know. Yes, we *know* it. The United States falls into grievous error by denying that knowledge, by denying reality.

This disposition to deny reality was cruelly in evidence at the Helsinki Conference of 1975, when thirty-five Western and Eastern countries concluded a kind of World War II peace settlement, the Final Act of the Conference on Security and Cooperation in Europe. This in effect gave recognition to Soviet conquests in return for Soviet-bloc agreement to a "basket" of "human rights" that each nation guaranteed its citizens, and, in varying degrees, the citizens of other signatories. The Soviets received recognition from the West of their new frontiers, but they never gave a moment's consideration to abiding by the commitment to "Cooperation in Humanitarian and Other Fields."

I first sought to describe this pattern of response at a Convocation of the Hebrew University of Jerusalem on July 5, 1976. I had been invited to receive an honorary degree, as had Axel Springer, the German publisher, and Andrei Sakharov. Sakharov was not there.

The Helsinki Accords—including the rights of travel and communication by citizens of the signatory states—were then just a year old. Already the Accords were unraveling. Sakharov had not been allowed to leave the

Soviet Union to travel to Jerusalem. So I spoke about the year that had followed the signing of the Accords on August 1, 1975: "In that year it has become unmistakably clear that the West was utterly deceived. The rulers of Soviet Russia solemnly signed an agreement . . . which they had not the least intention to abide by. One cannot take them much to task for this. They acted out of the purist Leninist doctrine that when dealing with the bourgeois powers it is both morally correct and politically necessary to lie, to cheat, to dissimulate, to deceive, practices which would succeed by virtue of bourgeois corruption and which would end by that class selling the rope with which it would be hung." The essence of the problem, I continued, Sakharov himself had addressed. "The rulers of Soviet Russia, brutalized as they are brutalizing, insular and often ignorant, the polar opposite of that which they protest with unfailing excess, may nonetheless lay claim to a singular perception which for sophistication and worldliness has no equal in the West. That is the perception that there persists in the West an irrational but at times seemingly indomitable desire to believe what the rulers of Soviet Russia say. . . . 'Detente without democratization,' Sakharov had written in 1973, 'would be very dangerous.'" *That* is precisely what we got. It is very much the source of our present danger.

The Helsinki Accords ought never to have been signed. There *was* no accord. When this became obvious, the United States and the other democracies at the very least should have stopped pretending. We did just the opposite. In two incredible conferences, first in Belgrade, then in Madrid (the latter lasting three years!), the signatories solemnly reviewed the progress they were making in upholding and securing the rights enunciated at Helsinki. The Final Act at Madrid, as an example, agreed to "respect the workers' right to freely set up labor unions, join them and enjoy the prerogatives that are recognized by international law. . . ." The foreign ministers of the thirty-five Western and Eastern nations had just gathered to sign the document as the authorities in Poland announced that they had dissolved the Union of Writers, one of the most prestigious organizations in that nation. The nominal reason? The union's membership had failed to agree to demands of the Communist minority within it that all writers should endorse Communist values in their work. That would suffice, but of course the most important reason was that the Writers' Union had steadfastly supported Solidarity, the first true trade union ever to be formed in a Communist nation—and to be recognized by the regime. Earlier in the year, Solidarity itself had been outlawed, this in absolute violation of the ILO treaties by which Poland was and is bound.

Consider that this took place two and a half years into the administration of President Reagan, a leader whose every public position would argue contempt for such self-deception, if not hypocrisy. Lech Walesa was barely out of prison, or what was in effect prison, his union smashed, his nation in the agony of freedom almost attained, and now lost. Yet, the United States solemnly agreed that the Polish regime respected "the workers' right to freely set up labor unions." To be sure, our Ambassador to the Madrid conference took audacity to its outer limits in addressing and stipulating the human rights violations of the totalitarians. But the question remains: Why were we there? We knew—did we not?—that they would lie and that we would nonetheless be persuaded we had to go along.

Shortly after the Final Act of Madrid was published, François de Rose, a former French Ambassador to the

North Atlantic Treaty Organization, expressed his be-
wilderment, contempt, concern. Every one of the guar-
antees in the Madrid Final Act, he noted, was nullified
by a clause providing that the rights listed were to be
exercised "in accordance with the legislation of the States
concerned." Eight years had passed since the initial
Helsinki Accords. In that time, Afghanistan had been
invaded, Sakharov exiled, Soviet dissenters, especially
those who sought to monitor the Helsinki agreements,
sent to "psychiatric hospitals"—all in accord with the
legislation of the state concerned. "It is a sad negation
of our own values," he wrote, "to pretend to attach so
much meaning to an exercise that is clearly nothing more
than a vast international hoax."

He is right. There is a question of honor here. And
when the totalitarian nations observe us acting without
honor, there is humiliation.

I return to the proposition that we seem somehow to
have lost our earlier belief that international relations—
and also to a degree the internal conduct of governments—can and should be governed by a regime of public
international law. If this statement can be thought of as
a question, then there is an answer. International law
exists. It is not an option. It is a fact. In our more ex-
pansive national moods, it has sometimes proved an in-
convenient fact. Early in Woodrow Wilson's presidency,
the Mexican general Victoriano Huerta overthrew the
legitimate (and liberal) government of Francisco I.
Madero, murdering him. Wilson was outraged, and accepted Bryan's counsel that a test of "constitutional legitimacy" would be applied to any Mexican government
seeking American recognition. John Bassett Moore at the
State Department would have none of it. Enunciating a
practice that began with Jefferson, and that generally
accords with customary international law, he pro-

nounced: "We regard governments as existing or not existing. We do not require them to be chosen by popular vote." That was the law. Convenient or not. And that is the point of law. Not least when dealing with such as Bryan and Wilson, who, whatever their lapses, wished to be lawful.

Consider that in the immediate aftermath of World War II the United States had the power more or less directly to restore the western part of Hitler's Germany to the political democracy it had once been. Where can it be said we have such power today? By contrast, the Soviet Union—which transformed East Germany into a regime of *its* design—continues to have the power to advance its ideological objectives. It can count its successes. More and more, it appears that Nicaragua is going to be one of those successes. It appears that Afghanistan will be another, for even if outright occupation does not persist indefinitely, a pro-Moscow, moderately Marxist-Leninist regime will remain. This disparity between the influence of the U.S. and the U.S.S.R. arises largely from the continuing, and perceptibly increasing, chaos in and between *new* nations. In 1982, the Indonesian scholar Soedjatmoko stated: "It is a sad fact that more than 100 wars have been fought in the Third World since the end of the Second World War, and most of them have been due to our own internal disagreements and tensions."

Crisis and chaos are conditions in which totalitarian purposes thrive. Or so such regimes judge. In Lenin's phrase, "the worse, the better." Following the Soviet invasion of Czechoslovakia in 1968, Vladimir Bolshakov, the Soviet propagandist and professional anti-Semite, wrote that ". . . at the request of many thousands of Czechoslovak Communists . . . the troops of five Warsaw Treaty countries rendered internationalist assistance to the fraternal Czechoslovak people in their struggle against the counter-revolution. . . ." There is a certain concession to Western form here—the assertion of treaty rights—but none of the substance.

The Soviets later proclaimed what came to be known as the Brezhnev Doctrine. In brief, this asserted that the Soviets would use armed force to "protect" Communist regimes already in power. More than a decade later, in January 1980, Boris Ponomarev set forth a strikingly similar proposition about the Third World, which I call the "Ponomarev Doctrine." Ponomarev, still a "Candidate Member" of the Politburo, the man who slaughtered unknown thousands of Spanish Communists and others who in the 1930s fled to "safety" in Russia, has been in charge of Soviet relations with non-Communist regimes since that time. (In effect, this means relations with the orthodox Communist party in those countries—and *always* there is such a party.) As a measure of growing confidence, or a sense of growing opportunity, or both, Ponomarev now proclaimed that the boundaries of "socialism's" concerns had expanded to include the nations of Asia, Africa, and Latin America. The Soviet Union, he implied, would no longer be doctrinally orthodox with respect to those it would support. If there were "fighters for true freedom" in these nations, that would qualify them for the support of "Marxist-Leninists and internationalists . . . they have the right to depend on our solidarity and support."

Need it be said that the one way *not* to counter this proposition is to emulate it? The Soviets have acquired proxy forces, principally those of Cuba and (more recently) elements of the armed forces and police of the German Democratic Republic, which they use to exploit such opportunities as present themselves. This is done in the usual lying and dissimulating manner. For the United States to respond in kind is a policy devoid alike of ethical authority, political promise, or legality. The question presses: Buffeted by outrage, and enraged by the contempt of adversaries for our standards, can we even so hold to those standards? Can we discern our interest in doing so?

Surely, we seem to have learned little from the "hostage crisis" of 1979–81. On November 4, 1979, our embassy in Tehran was seized by a political faction in that tumultuous nation. The bulk of the embassy staff remained in captivity for 444 days, until January 20, 1981—the moment a new President was inaugurated. For Americans generally, the holding of the hostages was an excruciating and protracted national humiliation. In the end, the personal valor of most of the Americans, and notably Chargé d'Affaires Bruce L. Laingen, somehow redeemed the experience. But little thanks for that was owed their government.

One returns to the idea of law. The first reaction in Washington to the seizure of our embassy was not that the law was being broken, but that we had somehow given offense. The President dispatched an envoy known for his sympathies for students and minorities. We would evidently discuss the matter—about which there was *nothing whatever* to discuss. There is no more fundamental tenet of international law than the immunity of ambassadors, and by extension of diplomatic personnel. It is embodied in the "extraterritorial" status of embassy buildings themselves. Indeed, it was the establishment of this obligation that made international relations possible. It is told that one of the ancient Persian emperors sent emissaries to Athens and to Sparta to proclaim his dominion over the sea and the land. The Athenians threw one envoy down a well; the Spartans buried the other alive. Whereupon in Sparta the auguries turned uniformly ominous, a great crime had been committed. At length two Spartan noblemen volunteered to travel to Persepolis to offer themselves in return for the murdered ambassadors. It is, lastly, related that the Persians declined the offer with disdain.

Twenty-five hundred years or so later, the United States, facing a not dissimilar situation, seemingly did not know its rights. Our response was political when it ought to have been legal. On November 9, we applied to the UN Security Council to "consider what might be done" to get our people and our embassy back. *This was not the business of the Security Council.* No threat to the peace was involved unless we chose to make one, which would create another situation altogether. What was required was that the Iranian government uphold the clearest prescription of international law. The Security Council dithered. Iranian authorities ignored all requests for restitution. The new year arrived. The United States pressed on the Security Council a resolution to impose a sweeping embargo on Iran. On January 13, with absolute predictability, the Soviet Union vetoed the resolution.

At minimum, it has to be said that the United States response to the seizure of the Tehran embassy was that of a nation unaccustomed to asking what bearing, if any, international law might have on an international crisis. It may be that this is nothing more than the fading of a nineteenth-century ethos. Or it may be other things: fecklessness, disillusion, inexperience. For certain, some of each quality was in evidence. The Department of State evidently had not prepared itself for this kind of crisis. In *The Year Book of World Affairs 1982*, Alfred P. Rubin, a professor at the Fletcher School of Law and Diplomacy, made the blunt assessment that during the Carter years the post of senior law officer of the State Department was filled by two successive incumbents, "neither of whom had any prior training, experience or manifest interest in international law."

It would appear that during the first weeks of the crisis no one in the administration thought of one obvious move: going to the International Court of Justice, where a prompt and unanimous decision in favor of the United States would certainly have been rendered, with all that would follow regarding American actions, including self-help. Rubin reports that on November 13 one of his former students, then on the professional staff of a Senate committee, called to ask if this was not the obvious course. He checked the relevant treaties. Both the United States and Iran had formally agreed, years earlier, that the Court would have jurisdiction in a matter such as that at hand. His colleague Leo Gross had done the same checking, and had reached the same conclusion. By November 15, Rubin was able to see the head of the Iranian task force. He presented the case for going to the Court, adding the subtle but powerfully important point, central to the efficacy of international law when it is invoked, that complying with a court order, other nations could bring pressure on Iran without seeming to side with the United States.

Rubin was indefatigable and passionate. He cared for his country, and his calling. Here was the clearest case that could come before the Court. A *real* case. (The reader should know that the Court doesn't have many. About two decisions a year are handed down; there are rarely more than five cases pending. It may be said without disrespect that the Court looks for work. This in a world where, according to the Rector of the United Nations University, there are roughly four wars a year among nonaligned nations alone!) Rubin was instrumental in inducing a *New York Times* editorial, which, however, suggested that Iran, yes, Iran, go to the Court, to obtain a judicial determination as to whether the United States was implicated in the alleged crimes of the Shah. This "garbled suggestion . . . so badly attuned to any reality," seemed to Rubin to make things even worse.

I suppose that I reveal my generation—graduate school just after World War II—when I say that, on learning of the seizure of the Tehran embassy, I simply assumed that recourse to the law would be the *first* response of the State Department. But then a week or so went by. No such response occurred. I called Leo Gross. Did I have it wrong? He assured me otherwise. I thereupon wrote a statement which I delivered in the Senate during morning hour of the day that *Times* editorial appeared. Rubin later wrote: "On . . . November 20, Senator Daniel Patrick Moynihan, a graduate of The Fletcher School who had been in direct contact with Professor Gross about the hostages situation, gave a speech on the Senate floor urging that the United States take the hostages situation to the International Court of Justice. While Professor Gross was convinced that the bureaucracy in the State Department was unmovable, he had concluded that pressure from Moynihan might have direct effects in the White House."

I may indeed have had a small effect—in part because it was a short speech. Possibly also because the position was correct. I said: "In the case of the illegal seizure of our Embassy in Iran, the United States has the clear opportunity to exercise its right under the optional protocol to the Geneva Convention of 1961 on diplomatic relations. . . . Mr. President, both Iran and the United States are parties to the convention and to the optional protocol which confers compulsory jurisdiction upon the International Court of Justice. . . . I suppose there will be those who ask, what can the International Court of Justice do? I can answer that with

. . . some precision. The International Court of Justice can say what is law and which party has violated it. The U.S. Government has put too much of its hopes and efforts into the rule of law to ignore the institution of the Court at this moment. . . . It would be the most prudent and immediate measure we could take. [It is] a far more appropriate forum . . . than the Security Council. I sometimes fear that [we have failed to address] the Court because it has been forgotten that the Court is there. . . . I simply urge the administration . . . to go . . . to the Court and exhibit in action its belief in the existence of international law. The world is tumbling into anarchy."

Nine days later, on November 29, the United States finally applied to the Court for relief—specifically for the return of all hostages, on behalf of all diplomatic premises, including full freedom of movement and protection of all persons attached to our embassy and consulate, no trial of any hostage, and no action by Iran that might prejudice further United States entitlements as judged by the Court. The next day the Court advised both nations that the matter was *sub judice,* under advisement. December 10 was set as the date for the parties to present their views on the request for interim measures. On December 15, a unanimous Court issued an interim order that met every United States position.

It had to. There *is* such a thing as international law. Clearly, Iran had violated it; clearly, the final decision in the case would uphold the rights of the United States completely. And the decision would *then* give us grounds for seeking action by the Security Council or the General Assembly—action, that is, to uphold a Court order—and not least grounds for taking military action under the doctrine of self-help. This is, roughly, the doctrine under which a nation can enforce its own rights, the more so when an international court has affirmed that those rights have been violated. The interim order further included this direction to Iran and the United States: While the issue was *sub judice,* nothing was to be done to make matters worse.

The International Court of Justice handed down its final decision on May 24, 1980. From the initial American application to final disposition had required less than six months. It was manifest from the first that the Court would act, and act quickly, and act entirely to our satisfaction and advantage. The final decision upheld the United States application on all points.

But it was too late. One month earlier, on April 24, the United States had launched the helicopter raid into Iran that failed. Later, the U.S. claimed self-defense before the Security Council. It is difficult to disagree with Rubin, who concludes: "Since the Order of provisional measures was not yet a 'decision,' and the judgment which would be a 'decision' was expected momentarily, the rescue mission amounted to the United States gambling on a military success that would in the longer run prove disastrous, or a failure that would in the short run remove from the hands of the United States the strongest tool it had to bring world pressure on Iran to release the hostages."

Enough has been made public about the rescue plan for its near recklessness to be clear. Simple math will take you there. Suppose a plan involves six successive steps, each of which must succeed in order for the next to succeed. Each step has a (very high) 90 percent probability of success. The overall operation then has about a fifty-fifty chance of making it. What was the thinking of those in Washington who would risk the lives of the airmen and other military personnel who were to carry out the raid, some of whom did die, and the lives of the hostages? For certain, this was not the thinking of persons who know much about international law or care much about it. In the Court's final decision, the Soviet member, Judge Morozov, rather enjoyed himself on this point. The regime of the Ayatollah Khomeini presumedly enjoyed itself most. It continued to hold the hostages until the exact moment when the man who had ordered the raid ceased to be President.

It would be pleasing to find that something was learned. Nothing was. In April of 1982, Argentina seized the Falkland Islands from Great Britain in a manner wholly in violation of the United Nations Charter. The validity of the Argentine claim to the "Malvinas" has nothing to do with the illegality of its action. Under the Charter, Argentina has forbidden itself the use of force in settling such disputes. The Charter forbids it, and Argentina of its own free will submitted to that restraint. Britain was entirely in the right, and free to take any action it wished. I spoke in the Senate urging that it take the case to the Court. This argument had enough force for *The Times* of London to report it. The point was identical to that of the hostage crisis. The Court would rule the Argentinian conduct illegal. Britain would thereupon be free to do as it would. If the United States then chose to support the British, *we* would be free to do so under color of the Court orders.

This is not cynicism masking as legalism. The United States is not obliged to get involved in every dispute around the globe, and obviously ought not. But when it does, the legitimate national interest is to do so successfully. In the Falklands, or Malvinas, dispute, we had the legitimate interest of retaining the good will of both nations. Instead, we risked both. First, we declared ourselves a friend of both parties. Finally, we supported Britain. Whereupon the Argentines felt betrayed. And, not incidentally, we muddled our case against Soviet interference in this hemisphere. (The Falklands were permanently occupied by Britain *after* the proclamation of the Monroe Doctrine.) A final observation from Professor Rubin: when we finally did support the British, "our position was made to appear politically expedient, not a matter of principle." None seemed to grasp that plain loyalty—to allies; to principles—is the highest politics, and ultimately the best.

Eighteen months later the scene shifts to another island, Grenada, just north and east of Trinidad. There American forces landed October 25, 1983, in order, in the first of many explanations, to secure the safety of Americans in the aftermath of a party coup in which the Marxist leader Maurice Bishop was deposed and murdered. If the American medical students, and other American nationals there, had been seriously threatened, and if American forces acted solely to rescue them (as Israeli forces rescued the hostages held at Entebbe airport in Uganda in 1976), a case could be made that international law gave us the right to invade. But our actual objective, soon proclaimed and achieved, was to replace the government there. We did not have this right. Article 18 of the Charter of the Organization of American States declares that no state has the right to intervene directly or indirectly, for any reason whatsoever, in the internal or external affairs of any other state. Thus we had a positive obligation not to do so.

An attempt was made to justify our action in terms of a treaty of mutual assistance entered into by a number of Windward Islands, including Grenada. Of this the director of the International Law Institute at Georgetown Law School, who thought the invasion justifiable, even so said the legal defenses offered "embarrass people who believe in law." But most striking was how few such defenses were offered. To the contrary, there was almost a preemptive strike by the President's supporters against any who would raise such irrelevancies. George Will, as learned and thoughtful a commentator as to be found, noted, correctly, that on the day of the invasion I "dropped into the Senate press gallery to charge that we may have violated the UN Charter." (In point of fact I said we had violated that of the OAS also.) Will continued: "But it is bad enough we pay for the United Nations; surely we do not have to pay attention to it." That is not a satisfactory retort. Paying attention to the UN Charter is paying attention to *our* understanding of the law of nations. This is what we are presumed to believe. Or formerly to have believed.

We seem to have come to regard international law as a self-imposed restraint that puts us at a disadvantage in a lawless world. A *Wall Street Journal* editorial at this time began by recounting a dinner table conversation in which a guest declared, "We are only going to be able to talk sensibly about Granada if anyone here who is an international lawyer agrees to keep his mouth shut." What is missing from this is the sense we once had that it is in our *interest* to advance the cause of law in world affairs. Certainly we continue to understand this with respect to our internal affairs. One can be worldly about this. It is obviously the interest of the "satisfied powers," as the term once was, to see that others abide by law, especially when the particular law has been devised by those particular powers. But this is not truly the case with the United Nations Charter. Its essential provisions were accepted as law long before the Charter was drafted. Besides, we are better than this. What does it mean to be an American if not to know that law in fact protects the weak. Above an entrance to the Department of Justice building on Pennsylvania Avenue (dating from the era of the Republican administrations of the 1920s when the Federal Triangle was built) will be found inscribed the plain injunction WHERE LAW ENDS, TYRANNY BE-GINS. Each of those presidents would have had us a member of the World Court. They thought it mattered. Seemingly, presidents no longer do. When the United Nations General Assembly voted massively to "deplore" our invasion—every NATO ally either voting against us or abstaining, and only eight nations in all voting with us—President Reagan was at lengths to have it under-stood that he could not care less. So much for world opinion which American presidents once thought would be the natural ally of American purposes.

James Reston remarked of President Reagan's state-ment on covert military action that "This is precisely what the Russians believe." And this is the problem here also. There is a rule: Organizations in conflict become like one another. It is said that as the Soviets despise interna-tional law, we have no choice but to dispense with it. In the Grenada situation there clearly was no point in going to the Security Council: *they* took *us* there. But was it out of the question to go to the OAS as we had done in the Dominican Republic invasion in 1965? There is no veto at the OAS.

It happens I was one of the last Americans to meet Maurice Bishop, the prime minister of Grenada whose execution on October 19 was followed by the landing of our forces six days later. Bishop had come to Washing-ton the previous June. Possibly he wanted a better re-lationship with the United States. He had surely done little to deserve this, but that is not the question. The question is whether it would have been in our interest to have some influence with his government, which was beginning, understandably, to be seen as a threat by its small, democratic neighbors. We met in my Senate office. He spoke in generalities. I responded in generalities. It occurred to me he thought his remarks were being recorded. I thereupon offered to see him off and took him on a two-block walk along the corridor to the opposite corner of the Russell Building. Immediately he confided that he was aware of the CIA plot to overthrow him. There was no such intrigue; no activity of any kind. I told him that; told him the Committees of the Congress would never allow it. I then went beyond any brief I might have had as a legislator. I said if I were he, I would not worry about the CIA, I would worry about the KGB. It was a simple enough thought. The Soviet system does not accommodate itself even to quasi-independent allies. Castro, by now, had been reduced to a pitiable condition, hiring out his army to the Soviets, in order to maintain his economy. I merely suggest that a nimble diplomacy would have suggested an approach to Havana, where clearly Castro was utterly shaken by Bishop's death. (He later stated that relations between Cuba and Bishop's successors in Grenada were "cold and tense.") The Soviets were not much pleased by this reaction. They canceled their national day reception, a high point in the routine of reaffirming Soviet-Cuban solidarity. Might we not have attempted to influence Cuba, a source of our problems in the Caribbean, rather than Grenada (population 115,000), a symptom? A decent respect for international law, *inter alia,* as international lawyers will say, might have occasioned a weekend's pause in which we could have considered our interests rather than merely giving in to our impulses. That, largely, is what law is about.